GOLF AT ST ANDREWS

GOLF AT

ST ANDREWS

Keith Mackie

FOREWORD BY JACK NICKLAUS

PELICAN PUBLISHING COMPANY
Gretna 1995

For Chris, Donna, Gail, and Ryan,
without whom life would have no meaning

Published simultaneously in April 1995 by
Pelican Publishing Company, Inc., in North America
Aurum Press Limited in the United Kingdom

ISBN 1-56554-129-4

This book has been designed and produced by Aurum Press Limited,
25 Bedford Avenue, London WC1B 3AT.

Designed by Robert Updegraff

Printed in China
Published by Pelican Publishing Company, Inc.
1101 Monroe Street, Gretna, Louisiana 70053

CONTENTS

FOREWORD

In a significant way my golf was shaped by the traditions and history of Scotland right from the beginning. I learned to play the game on a course designed by Donald Ross, who once worked with Old Tom Morris at St Andrews, and, right from my earliest days, I have always felt a distinct affinity with the traditions that shaped this wonderful game. So, long before I ever set foot on Scottish soil, it had become clear to me that winning the world's oldest championship at the birthplace of the game would be a great achievement.

By 1970 I had already experienced the thrill of winning the Open at Muirfield; but I arrived early for the Championship at St Andrews and worked hard to get to know the Old Course more intimately and to bring my game to a peak.

Even so, on the last green I felt it had all slipped away – until Doug Sanders missed a short putt to beat me. I hate to see anyone lose a title like that, and felt great compassion for Doug, but at the same time could not deny the sense of relief that I had been given another chance to achieve my outstanding ambition.

The next afternoon I had a downhill putt of about seven feet to win the Open, and when it dropped I reacted in a manner I had never experienced before – or since. Without knowing what I was doing, I leapt in the air and tossed my putter high over my head in a spontaneous release of tension and emotion, which said everything about my desire to win at the Home of Golf.

But St Andrews has given me much more than that unforgettable moment and the equally gratifying victory when the Open returned in 1978. The genuine warmth and friendliness of the St Andrews people is second to none. I have been made an honorary member of the Royal and Ancient and the St Andrews Golf Club; these are privileges I cherish. All in all, I have a real sense of belonging, not just in the St Andrews of the present, but also of the past, a close bond with our golfing ancestors and their great achievements.

Because of my affection for the place, I am delighted that Keith Mackie has produced such a wide-ranging new book about St Andrews. This book traces not only the evolution of the famous links and the town, but the creation of the Royal and Ancient Golf Club, the changes in equipment used throughout the centuries, the great championships and the players who won them, the caddies, the personalities, the frustrations and the humour of our marvellous game. Other books have examined single aspects of St Andrews. This one covers the full, broad canvas in fascinating detail.

Keith is exceptionally well qualified to tell this story. He comes from an old-established St Andrews family, and has been writing about the game for as long as I have been playing professionally. He first interviewed me as a rookie professional in 1962. We travelled together to an event at Hillside in Lancashire and our paths continue to cross at the great championships, from St Andrews to Augusta, and in many odd golfing corners of the world.

For those who do not know the Home of Golf first-hand, reading *Golf at St Andrews* will sharpen the appetite for a visit. For those who do, it will stir many vivid and pleasant memories.

Jack Nicklaus

PREFACE

Some of my earliest memories are of golf talk, the air rich with the smell of my grandfather's pipe tobacco as he and my father recalled shots hit into the heart of the green and putts holed. I was hooked long before I ever set foot on a golf course.

My father was a son of St Andrews, a professional and an accomplished clubmaker and I was fortunate enough to be literally born into the game. Learning to grip a club came as easily as walking. The traditions and etiquette of golf were absorbed with every breath.

Very quickly, I learned that golf is more than a game. It has come to represent a standard of behaviour that is rapidly disappearing from most other sports, and from life itself. The very essence of golf is the emphasis it places on personal integrity. Every golfer in every round has the chance to cheat without fear of being found out – yet the vast majority resist the temptation, realizing that it is an offence not only against an opponent, but against themselves and the game itself.

Within this framework of self-imposed discipline the exact appeal of golf is hard to define. Arnold Palmer has come as close as anyone to capturing it in words: 'It is deceptively simple and endlessly complicated. A child can play it well, and a grown man can never master it. Any single round is full of unexpected triumphs and seemingly perfect shots that end in disaster. It is almost a science, yet it is a puzzle without an answer. It is gratifying and tantalizing, precise and unpredictable.'

No less important is the fact that golf has retained the spirit of conviviality that characterized its infancy in Scotland more than 600 years ago; the ritual of animated post-mortem discussion over a few glasses is still something without which any round of golf is incomplete.

All these golfing pleasures have been the birthright of the citizens of St Andrews for many generations; and they are pleasures which they increasingly share with players from an ever-growing list of golfing nations. Happily golf is renowned for its ability to transcend any barriers of age or ability. It also leaps the obstinate hurdle of language, allowing genuine warmth and affinity to grow between players whose only means of communication is the one word 'golf'. Nowhere is this more true than at the birthplace of the game. In this book I have tried to give a flavour of St Andrews through the centuries, of the way it has influenced the development and growth of our marvellous game, and of the champions who have triumphed over its ancient fairways.

Good fortune has given me the chance to play golf in many parts of the world, to witness the major championships and enjoy the game with many of the leading players, but all this pales into insignificance on a spring morning on the Old Course with the ball soaring white and clean against heather and sky and the sun glinting on a smudge of snow in the distant Grampian Mountains. Nowhere can the game be played with more pleasure than on the fairways that brought it to life.

The old grey city which is virtually a second home to golfers from all over the world.

KEITH MACKIE
St Andrews
November 1994

Chapter 1

THE HOME OF GOLF

THE OLD COURSE AT ST ANDREWS, undoubtedly the most famous golf course in the world, has been witness to the entire history of the game, which has been played over the undulating linksland on the northern borders of the city for more than 600 years without interruption. This sandy soil has felt the tread of every great champion; it has flinched as millions of golfers down the centuries have hammered and hacked, swiped and swished at balls of wood, leather, gutta percha and balata; it has felt the caress of hand-crafted clubs of hickory and blackthorn and suffered the sharp assault of today's flashing blades of steel and titanium.

St Andrews was the stage upon which, as the popularity of the game spread south of the border, the Scots champions were first challenged by the English. Later, it played host to the fast improving golfers of the New World, who were followed, in turn, by those of Europe, South Africa, Australasia, South America and, most recently, Japan and China. There is no other place that has had such a far-reaching and longstanding influence on a great sport.

The written rules of the game were, it is true, first set down in Edinburgh, and the Open Championship was first established at Prestwick, but such precedents do not affect the pre-eminence of the old, grey cathedral city. For the unchanging challenge of the Old Course, and the unchallenged authority of the Royal and Ancient Golf Club which overlooks the historic links, have long established St Andrews' claim to the title of the Home of Golf – in truth, it was the very cradle of the game.

Such is the prestige and eminence enjoyed by St Andrews that every devotee of the game from Yonkers to Yokohama, from Moscow to Melbourne, taking in all nine-hole and eighteen-hole stops along the way, aspires to play the Old Course. Each year the city's broad streets and narrow wynds reverberate to the languages of the world as golfing pilgrims come to test their skills against the ghosts of Old Tom Morris and Bobby Jones; to place their feet on the worn stones of the Swilcan Bridge, where every champion in the history of the game has crossed on the way to the final green. What these visitors discover here is an atmosphere so tangible as to be almost claustrophobic, a sense of living history, and a vista which has

This painting, believed to date from about 1720, shows golfers on what would subsequently become the Old Course. Then, as now, the city and the West Sands provided a spectacular backdrop to the scene.

RIGHT *Golfers approaching the first green in about 1890.* BELOW *A group of nineteenth-century players by the Swilcan Burn, clearly taken earlier than the photograph above as the stream is as yet unembanked.*

excited golfers for six centuries. In the wind- and sun-burnished turf of the Old Course are reflected not only the glorious history of the game, but a seemingly endless and challenging future.

How did St Andrews achieve this position of pre-eminence, this almost mystical hold on the collective subconscious of the golfing community?

To answer that question it is necessary to go back to the very origins of the game, or as close to them as it is possible to get with any accuracy.

Golf is reputed to have been a popular pastime when St Andrews University was founded in 1413. Certainly it was well enough established forty years later for King James II to ban it by Act of the Scottish Parliament in 1457. The ban was thought necessary because any citizen who was fit enough to swing a golf club was required by law to practise with the long bow, which was an essential part of Scotland's defences against the constant incursions of the English. It seems likely that, if golf had so gripped the imagination of fifteenth-century Scots that national safety required its prohibition, its origins must lie even further back in the history of the kingdom. Unfortunately, however, no written evidence survives from any earlier date – or none that has, as yet, been unearthed.

ABOVE *The 1457 Act of the Scottish Parliament which banned the playing of 'fute-ball, golfe, or other sik unprofitable sportes'.* LEFT *St Andrews University, Scotland's oldest, provided the basis of the city's prosperity in the Middle Ages and continues to be a major centre of learning today.*

It is, however, beyond doubt that, in those early days, golf was a pastime restricted to the east coast of Scotland, roughly between Aberdeen and Edinburgh. In this region the sea, receding from the rich arable land, had left behind an area of sand dunes with a thin covering of topsoil which nurtured fine-bladed, deep-rooted grass. This sward afforded no more than sparse grazing for a few sheep or goats, but proved an ideal breeding ground for rabbits. It also provided the perfect site for the archery butts, for football – and for golf.

Scotland was not, of course, the first place where people played with sticks and balls; every civilization from earliest times has developed some form of such games. The Romans played *paganica*, the Chinese game was called *suigan* and the Dutch got excited about *kolven*. It is from the Netherlands that the strongest and most persistent claims to have originated golf can still be heard. Indeed, well into the twentieth century many Scots were convinced that their game had been imported across the North Sea by the crews of the ships which plied regular passage between the Low Countries and the bustling ports of Leith and St Andrews.

There are certainly references to a club-and-ball game being played at the Dutch village of Loenen in 1296, but it is not described in sufficient detail for it to be classed as a form of proto-golf. Later illustrations of the Dutch game show it being played on small areas of land rather like bowling greens – and also on frozen canals in winter. This does not suggest a game that was very golf-like – imagine the winner being the player who was successful in knocking his ball through a hole in the ice in the least number of strokes, and thus losing it forever. The game can be frustrating enough without adding penalties like that!

By contrast, the game to which east coast Scots became so addicted in the early 1400s, and possibly during the century before, bears a striking and direct resemblance to the game which is played throughout the world today. The aim was to play the ball from a teeing area into a distant hole in the least number of strokes, each successive shot being played from

Hell bunker on the fourteenth hole of the Old Course in about 1840.

where the ball came to rest. But the implements used would seem very unfamiliar to the modern player, and so would the courses.

Early balls would have been round stones gathered from the shore. Clubs would have been no more sophisticated than a suitably shaped branch of wood. Later, balls were fashioned from wood, then from leather stuffed with goose feathers, and purpose-built clubs were crafted from two pieces of wood – a shaft and a head – by artisans skilled in making bows.

The first courses were simply any patch of land which a particular golfer or group of golfers thought might be sporty and challenging. Ten groups of golfers playing over a large expanse of linksland might well choose ten different layouts; only when the numbers of golfers increased did everyone gradually come to accept the idea of a permanent, established course.

Courses could have any number of holes and they were designed almost instantly. A distant patch of short grass, perhaps conveniently cropped by a tethered goat, would be selected as the first green, a hole cut in the turf, and it was ready for play. The early links at Leith had only five holes. St Andrews had 22. Anyone equipped with a club and ball could play. There were no restrictions, no fees to pay, and always a nearby tavern where wagers were settled and new challenges issued. From its earliest days golf was not only a sport but a social occasion as well.

A busy scene on the Old Course in the late nineteenth century, with the mouth of the Swilcan Burn in the background.

It was not until nearly 300 years after the imposition of James II's short-lived ban on the game that golf became formalized in any way. This dramatic turning point in the game's development came about when 'gentlemen of honour skilful in the ancient and healthful exercise of the golf' requested the Magistrates and Council of Edinburgh to present a silver golf club to be played for in an annual competition over the links at Leith. The beautifully handwritten minutes of the meeting which approved the gift on 7 March 1744 are carefully preserved in the archives of the Scottish capital. They spell out in great detail the conditions under which 'Noblemen or Gentlemen or other Golfers from any part of great Britain or Ireland' could enter the annual event on payment of five shillings. The silver club was valued at £50 and the entry money was 'solely to be at the disposal of the victor'.

Having organized the event, the gentlemen of honour, who were later to adopt the title of The Honorable Company of Edinburgh Golfers and to create the classic championship links at Muirfield, had to commit the rules of play to paper. In thirteen succinctly worded rules, under the title 'Articles and Laws in Playing Golf' (The Rules of the Gentlemen Golfers, 1744), they set down the guidelines by which they played their own matches. Some 250 years later those rules still form the basis of the way the game is played worldwide – although they now run to 75 pages.

The minutes in the Edinburgh archives are the earliest recorded evidence of golfers forming themselves together in an official club or society, but the example of the capital was soon followed elsewhere in Scotland. St Andrews joined the list ten years later when 22 noblemen and gentlemen of the Kingdom of Fife formed the Society of St Andrews Golfers. They played their first annual challenge for a silver club on 14 May 1754.

The original rules of golf, as set down by the Honorable Company of Edinburgh Golfers in 1744.

The rules they used for that contest were those written out by the Gentlemen Golfers of Edinburgh ten years before:

1   You must tee your ball within a club's length of the hole.

2   Your tee must be on the ground.

3   You are not to change the ball which you strike off the tee.

4   You are not to remove stones, bones or any break club for the sake of playing your ball, except upon the fair green, and that only within a club's length of the ball.

5   If your ball comes among watter, or any wattery filth, you are at liberty to take out your ball and bringing it behind the hazard and teeing it, you may play it with any club and allow your adversary a stroke for so getting out your ball.

6   If your balls be found anywhere touching one another you are to lift the first ball till you play the last.

7   At holling you are to play your ball honestly at the hole, and not to play upon your adversary's ball, not lying in your way to the hole.

8   If you should lose your ball, by its being taken up, or any other way, you are to go back to the spot where you struck last and drop another ball and allow your adversary a stroke for the misfortune.

9   No man at holling his ball is to be allowed to mark his way to the hole with his club or anything else.

10 If a ball be stopp'd by any person, horse, dog, or any thing else, the ball so stopp'd must be played where it lyes.

11 If you draw your club in order to strike and proceed so far in the stroke as to be bringing down your club, if then your club should break in any way, it is to be accounted a stroke.

12 He whose ball lyes farthest from the hole is obliged to play first.

13 Neither trench, ditch, or dyke made for the preservation of the links, nor the Scholar's Holes or the soldier's lines shall be accounted a hazard but the ball is to be taken out, teed and play'd with any iron club.

The 'scholar's holes' and 'soldier's lines' were obviously hazards peculiar to the links at Leith, yet were still included in the rules used in St Andrews.

The members of the Society of St Andrews Golfers continued to play over the 22 holes of the course which ran northwards from the town along the edge of the West Sands, taking

Bunker problems for a mid-nineteenth-century golfer.

their place on the public links among golfers of all classes and abilities, just as they had before the formation of their society. Their more senior counterparts in Edinburgh were not so lucky. Their home course at Leith had only five holes and soon became impossibly overcrowded, forcing a switch to the public nine holes at nearby Musselburgh. But they were on the move again in the last decade of the nineteenth century, finally creating their own private course at Muirfield in 1891.

Thus, while the old-established Edinburgh clubs were seeking permanent homes – Bruntsfield had also quit its public course close to the castle and found land for a private club outside the city – the Old Course at St Andrews, and what had by then become the Royal and Ancient Golf Club, remained unchanged. It was this sense of robust continuity that gradually focused the attention of the ever-expanding golfing world on the small, grey city in Fife rather than the Scottish capital, where the (admittedly older) clubs were suffering a certain loss of identity. As a result, when the senior clubs agreed in 1897 that a uniform code of rules should be formulated, a unanimous decision was taken to entrust the task to the Royal and Ancient.

Similar considerations guided the development of the Open Championship. Although Prestwick, on the west coast of Scotland, had conceived the idea of the championship in 1860 and had held it at their own course until 1872, the staging of the event was subsequently shared on a rota basis with Edinburgh and St Andrews. Over the years the list of venues grew until, by the time of the First World War, a total of no less than 26 golf clubs had formed a consortium to run the Open. Such a system was extremely cumbrous and in 1919 the clubs involved agreed, without dissent, to place both the Amateur and the Open Championships in the hands of the Royal and Ancients at St Andrews.

St Andrews' status as the Home of Golf, and the position of the Royal and Ancient as the leading golf club, were thus firmly established, and have never subsequently been challenged.

The city of St Andrews takes its name from the apostle, no doubt as a consequence of certain of his bones and relics having been brought to the shores of Fife, where they were housed in the small church of St Mary-on-the-Crag overlooking what is now St Andrews harbour. The remains of that church still exist today, but fact and fantasy mingle when we seek an account of how the precious relics came to this then remote outpost of Christendom. Popular legend tells of a two-year journey by a Greek monk, Regulus, who had been instructed in a vision to take certain bones of St Andrew from the monastery of Patras and to journey to a far-distant island. His intrepid voyage supposedly came to an end when his open boat was wrecked in St Andrews Bay in about AD 390. Historical evidence, on the other hand, tends to suggest that the bones later authenticated as being those of St Andrew had been brought north by a bishop fleeing from England in about AD 750.

Legends are always more fun than facts, but by whatever route they travelled the relics of St Andrew were believed to have miraculous powers and they drew pilgrims from all parts of the known world to the rapidly growing community on the shores of the North Sea. St Andrew was promoted to be the patron saint of Scotland and the town named after him became the religious centre of the country, growing in size, prestige and wealth, and controlled with a rod of iron by its bishops.

St Andrews harbour; many early caddies were also fishermen and the harbour is still in use as a fishing port today.

19

The linksland on which the golf courses were to take shape was granted to the bishops by a charter of King David I in 1123 and, long before their thoughts began to turn to frivolous pastimes like golf, the local people were ranging freely over the links to snare rabbits and birds, and to cut turf to roof their homes and low quality peat for their fires. Since that initial charter a succession of grants of privilege and confirmations of charters have been granted by kings, archbishops and bishops – all protecting the right of the citizens of St Andrews to make use of the grassy linksland for 'golff, futball, schuting at al gamis with all uther maner of pastyme as ever thai pleis' as Archbishop Hamilton expressed it in a confirmation order of 25 January 1552.

As early as 1691 St Andrews was described as 'the metropolis of golfing' and the first minute of the Society of St Andrews Golfers in 1754 refers to the town as the 'alma mater' of golf. It was certainly popular with a succession of monarchs and Mary Queen of Scots is known to have played the links on many occasions. Indeed, her addiction to the game fuelled the accusations that she had been involved in the murder of her husband. A report of

An aerial view showing all the courses with the town and the Royal & Ancient clubhouse in the foreground and the Eden estuary in the distance – for a key to the photograph see the map on page 183.

A sketch of the town seen across the Swilcan Burn in the early nineteenth century; the walled road in the background is now a street lined with shops, houses and a hotel.

the time recounts that 'A few days after the murder ... she was seen openly exercising with pall mall and golf and at night plainly abusing her body with the Earl of Bothwell.'

The bishops who controlled the city of St Andrews in the years when it was the ecclesiastical centre of Scotland were also keen golfers. So, too, were the staff of the university. With its leading citizens showing the way, and with influential supporters of the game making regular visits to the city it is not surprising that St Andrews established an early reputation as a centre of golf.

As the all-pervading power of the Church waned, the administration of St Andrews eventually devolved to a Town Council which regularly issued commercial leases for areas of the links not used for golf. But they were always careful to protect the golfing rights. In a 1726 contract to allow rabbit breeding, for example, they stipulated: 'It is agreed that the part of the Links as presently golfed upon shall be kept entire and not ploughed up by the Town Council or their tenants.'

By this time, however, St Andrews was heading for a lengthy period of poverty and decay and the resolve of the Town Council to protect the rights of the citizens was ultimately put to the test – and found sadly lacking.

The early prosperity of the town had been based on its importance as a place of pilgrimage and as the site of Scotland's first university. With the Reformation and the loss of the Catholic Church's power and influence, much of St Andrews' *raison d'être* disappeared. By the eighteenth century the town was in decline and strong moves were underway to transfer the university to Perth. The decline was noted by travellers such as Dr Samuel Johnson, who after his visit in 1773 wrote of St Andrews as:

A city which only history shows to have once flourished. One of its streets is now lost and in those that remain there is the silence and solitude of inactive indigence and gloomy depopulation.

21

The ruins of St Andrews Cathedral. Consecrated in 1318, the building fell into decay in the seventeenth and eighteenth centuries and much of the stone was removed by the townspeople for re-use as building material.

The magnificent cathedral, consecrated in 1318 in a ceremony led by Bishop Lamberton and attended by Scotland's heroic King Robert the Bruce, lay in ruins, the stones carried away to help rebuild decaying houses.

It was against this background that the Town Council drew up an extraordinary eight-page contract granting a 50-year lease for mining rights on the links. On 8 September 1785 the Provost, Councillors and Magistrates of St Andrews signed a document which gave extensive rights to Charles Beaumont of Edinburgh. He was empowered to explore for coal, metals and minerals on 'All and every part of the lands of Pilmor Links ... and environs round the city'. He was also given:

> Full power and liberty to enter and break the surface in the said lands for the winning working obtaining getting and away carrying of coals and all other metals and minerals ... all to be done entirely on his own expenses and risque.

The lease goes on to spell out Beaumont's rights of access, including the right to construct roads for horses and carts if necessary, and the right to erect buildings and to pile up coal extracted from the area. He was, however, expressly prohibited and debarred from working *under* any part of the town, though he was given power 'To carry two or three different mines *through* such parts of the town from North to South in such places as he shall find expedient.' Some small protection was given to the golf course. Beaumont was not at liberty to:

> break the surface of the ground of the present track of the golf links, but that otherways he shall have full power and liberty to work for coals and all other metals under ground to as great extent as he pleases.

Fifty pounds a year or one tenth part of the proceeds of the gross sales of anything he discovered was the price Beaumont was asked to pay. Although much coal was successfully mined to the west and south of St Andrews during that period, the linksland, with water levels only a few feet below the sandy surface, was never likely to prove productive and there are no further records of Beaumont progressing with his ambitious scheme – much to the relief of golfers then and now.

But 12 years later the Town Council's need drove it to enter into another agreement which almost destroyed the golfing heritage of St Andrews. In January 1797, in a desperate bid to raise money, they offered the links as security against a loan. The continuing decline in the fortunes of the city meant that the loan could not be repaid when it fell due and the links were sold, passing into the hands of local merchants Charles and Cathcart Dempster.

Although the golfing area was protected in the deeds of sale, the wealthy father and son decided to turn the links into a commercial breeding ground for rabbits. Control of the animals was difficult and inevitably the golf course began to suffer. The ensuing battles between the Dempsters, the Town Council, and local golfers were heated and prolonged, leading to exchanges of blows, bitter words and legal documents.

The situation was saved by George Cheape, the Laird of Strathtyrum, an area of land on the outskirts of St Andrews with views across the golf courses to the sea. He bought the disputed links from the Dempsters with the sole intention of preserving the area for golf. Cheape was a keen playing member of the Society of St Andrews Golfers and he was true to his word. From 1821 until 1893, he and his descendants kept the links free of all commercial dealings and available to the citizens of St Andrews for golf and all other recreational activities.

OVERLEAF *The roof tops of the old grey city as seen from the tower of St Rule's church.*

BELOW *A panoramic view of the city, with the ruins of the cathedral in the foreground and the Eden estuary in the distance, beyond the golf courses and the West Sands.*

By the last decade of the nineteenth century St Andrews was once again entering a period of prosperity and the popularity of golf was such that both the Town Council and the Royal and Ancient agreed that a second course should be built. The club wanted a private course for use by their members; the Council and the majority of residents felt that a second public course was more appropriate. So there were two rival buyers for the land still owned by the Cheape family.

The Council bid £4,500, but in September 1893 James Cheape accepted the £5,000 offered by the Club and all the linksland west and north of the Swilcan Burn and as far as the estuary of the River Eden became the property of the private club. So anxious were the locals to regain and protect their ancient golfing rights that the Council promoted a Bill through Parliament in London. The resultant Links Act of 1894 authorized the Town Council to buy the Links back from the Royal and Ancient for £5,000 – exactly what they had paid for the land only a few months before. Under the terms of the Act the St Andrews Links were to be managed by a greens committee heavily weighted in favour of the Club, who were to have five members while the Council could nominate only two. But all regulations about starting times and play over the course agreed by the committee had to be submitted to the Council for approval. In addition, the Club undertook to build an additional eighteen holes, which to this day is called the New Course.

Up to this time golf at St Andrews had been free to everyone, citizen and visitor alike; but the 1894 Act authorized the charging of fees for the first time. Locals and members of the Royal and Ancient still enjoyed free golf, and so did visitors, except on the New Course in the months of July, August and September when a daily charge of two shillings and sixpence (about twelve pence in today's currency) was imposed. A weekly ticket cost about 42 pence. Unaccountably, the Old Course remained free to all-comers throughout the year.

A second Links Act was approved in 1913, by which time a third course – the Jubilee – had taken shape close to the three-mile expanse of the West Sands. The new Act withdrew the right of visitors to play the courses free and for the first time green fees were charged on all courses, but still not to the citizens of St Andrews and Royal and Ancient members. The Town Council was also given the go-ahead to acquire further land for the construction of a fourth course – the Eden – which was completed in 1913.

By the end of the Second World War, the Royal and Ancient could no longer bear the costs of maintaining the Old and New Courses which had been imposed on them many years earlier. The Council were forced to make a contribution, and they put another Act through Parliament which authorized them to make charges against citizens of St Andrews and members of the Royal and Ancient for play on the town's four courses. The maximum charge allowed by the Act was set at £2 per year, but the Council sought to minimize the resultant outcry by imposing only a £1 fee. Even so, when this was subsequently doubled a few years later the increase was described in the local paper as 'iniquitous'.

When the Town Council was eventually disbanded by sweeping local government re-organization, a further Act of Parliament, passed in 1974, established a Links Trust to take over the running of the courses and the protection of the links area for golf.

Recent developments at the ancient Home of Golf have once again aroused local hostility. In the 1980s the Links Trust decided to expand and upgrade the facilities at St Andrews in anticipation of the golfing needs of the twenty-first century. Both the Jubilee and Eden courses have been significantly redesigned and lengthened. A fifth course, the short Strathtyrum –

This sketch of 1875 shows a golfer and his caddy at the far end of the Old Course, with the Eden estuary in the background.

built on land bought from the family of the man who was responsible for saving the courses for the people of St Andrews in 1821 – has been opened, together with a nine-hole course, practice area, driving range, and clubhouse.

Controversy was aroused by the imposition of the new facilities on the ancient linksland, changing the historic views which are so much a part of its attraction for visitors and so fiercely cherished by residents. The panoramic view from the eighteenth green, which embraces the sweep of St Andrews Bay and the far reaches of the Old Course is now dominated by the new clubhouse, and the driving range encroaches to within a few yards – and is in full sight and sound – of the sixteenth hole.

Golfers from around the world may feel that, in providing modern amenities in such prominent, eye-catching positions, St Andrews is somehow chipping away at its own heritage – the legacy left by centuries of golf which is also the prime attraction for most of the visitors to the city. Yet despite these changes, St Andrews is still unique. The first and last holes of the Old Course are still played in full public view, under the windows of clubs, shops and hotels. Children with bags of clubs draped carelessly over their shoulders still ride through the streets, streets in which colourful golf shirts and sweaters outnumber business suits one hundred to one. Every waitress, barman, bank clerk and taxi-driver in the city is able to discuss the merits of the game – and probably plays it to a low handicap.

The challenge of the Old Course itself is constant, but only in its ever-changing nature – benign at one moment, fierce and demanding the next. The breeze can switch direction in an instant, giving a free ride for the full round or just as easily opposing at every hole. And it is still possible, when the final putt has been holed across the sloping expanse of the eighteenth green, to walk a few steps to the nearest bar and a sympathetic audience of fellow golfers. In that respect St Andrews has changed not at all in six centuries.

Chapter 2

BOTH ROYAL AND ANCIENT

I N THE MID-EIGHTEENTH CENTURY Scotland was a nation divided in the terrible aftermath of the Jacobite rising of 1745 and the massacre at Culloden, that fateful field where more than twelve hundred of Bonnie Prince Charlie's five thousand poorly equipped men, outnumbered almost two to one by the English-led forces, perished. In the months after the battle, Parliament in London debated the possibility of sterilizing all Jacobite women and destroying all seed corn north of the Highland Line so as to extirpate the inhabitants of the accursed country. Even a decade later Highlanders were still being hunted down by government troops, their cattle confiscated and their homes burned. They were forbidden to wear traditional dress or to carry arms. The penalty was instant death. This inhumane treatment was handed out to all Highlanders, regardless of whether they had been supporters of the uprising or not. It started a mass exodus to the New World, where the American fight for independence was still more than two decades away, and left a legacy of bitterness which is not wholly expunged, even two and a half centuries later.

But in Scotland's peaceful lowlands the horrors that were being perpetrated only a few miles to the north might as well have been taking place on another planet; by 1754 the grandees of St Andrews society had turned their minds away from politics and back to the comforts and pleasures of their city – among the chief of which was, of course, golf.

We may, perhaps, allow ourselves to imagine the scene that was enacted in one of the city's taverns one evening in the early months of that year. Very likely the cold wind from the North Sea which still buffets the low cliffs by the castle at this season would have rattled the windows of the back room where 22 noblemen and gentlemen of the Kingdom of Fife had gathered. Seated under the low ceiling, pitching their voices against the sounds of revelry which drifted through the smoke-filled atmosphere from the bar, these local notables would, no doubt, have soon settled in for a convivial evening and it was probably not long before their conversation would have turned to their favourite game. We do not know who first raised the question of creating a formal association along the lines of that instituted by their contemporaries in Edinburgh; but, however it came about, by the end of what was probably a long evening's drinking the Society of St Andrews Golfers had sprung into being.

Sir John Whyte-Melville, first elected captain of the Royal and Ancient Golf Club in 1823. The portrait, painted in 1874, shows him in the uniform of an R & A member, a red coat with yellow buttons. He died shortly after being elected captain for a second time in 1883.

The silver club for which the Noblemen and Gentlemen of St Andrews subscribed in 1754 and for which they agreed to compete each year.

The humble beginnings of what has since become the world's most powerful and famous golf club were recorded in a firm hand and have been preserved to this day. Under the 22 names of those present it states:

> The Noblemen and Gentlemen above named being admired of the Ancient and healthful exercise of the Golf, and at the same time having the interest and prosperity of the ancient city of St Andrews at heart, being the Alma Mater of the Golf, did in the year of our Lord 1754 contribute for a Silver club having a St Andrew engraved on the head thereof to be played for on the Links of St Andrews upon the fourteenth day of May said year, and yearly in time coming subject to the conditions and regulations following.

The founders of the Society were, no doubt, aware of the example set by the Gentlemen Golfers of Leith some ten years earlier. But it is also possible that the rationale behind the formation of the Society may have owed as much to its founders' commercial acumen as to their avowed purpose of enjoying good golf, good food and good liquor in each others' company.

As already noted, the middle of the eighteenth century was a period of decline for the ancient city. The reformation had robbed it of its leadership in church matters and the university was short of funding and in danger of being moved to Perth. In this context, the phrase: 'having the interest and prosperity of the ancient city of St Andrews at heart' suggests that the society was not simply an excuse for regular golf and its social aftermath, but that the 22 founders had some wider purpose in mind. Had they realized that St Andrews' pre-eminence as a golfing centre was slipping away towards Edinburgh? Were they trying to boost the dwindling number of golfing visitors to the city?

Whatever their motives, over the next century and a half they succeeded in turning a small private society into the world's most influential golf club. Today their successors have responsibility for administering the rules of the game in every country except the United States and Mexico, where the United States Golf Association holds sway, although the two bodies work closely together and have operated a common code for many years. They also have sole charge of the Open Championship, which they run with minimal staff and great efficiency.

In the early years of the Society, the captain for the year was simply the winner of the silver club towards the purchase of which the founders had subscribed; the first to gain this honour being William Landale, a merchant of St Andrews. The founding members of the society had access to the links of St Andrews, but no clubhouse. The popular inn run by Baillie Glass was the centre of their activities and an extract from the club records in 1766 instructs members to meet:

> once every fortnight by eleven o'clock and to play around the Links. To dine together at Baillie Glass and to pay each a shilling for his dinner – the absent as well as the present.

Then, as now, golf was a sociable game, almost as much attention being paid to the off-course activities as to the round itself. In the fashion of the day the members wore a uniform of red coats with yellow buttons. Committee members were allowed to be a little more flamboyant, with red frock coats and dark-blue velvet capes embroidered with silver club and ball. Dinners were usually lavish affairs with up to five meat courses and a corresponding quantity of wine. Claret was the popular drink of the time and Tobias Smollett recorded that club golfers rarely retired to bed with less than a gallon of it in their bellies. During the course of the meal, wagers on the day's matches would be paid – almost always in the form of bottles rather than money – and fresh challenges issued.

Pint bottles of claret appear to have been the accepted currency of the society, and most fines imposed on members for infringing the rules, not wearing the proper uniform, for example, would be paid in liquid form. If the captain missed a meeting he was automatically fined two bottles and in one particularly fractious week in 1779 five members were fined one bottle each 'for reflecting on the secretary', and another suffered the same penalty after having the audacity to order hot water.

By 1833, the popularity of golf, and the fame and standing of the Society of St Andrews Golfers, had so increased that the monarch of the day, William IV, bestowed his patronage upon the Society and it became the Royal and Ancient Golf Club, or, to golfers everywhere, simply the R & A. It is, however, worth noting that, in this, as in other matters, St Andrews cannot claim absolute priory. The Perth Golfing Society had been similarly honoured a year earlier.

By comparison with the game played on today's strictly controlled and well maintained courses, golf in those early days was a relatively rough and ready affair. Anyone with club and ball could play the Old Course. When the Society of St Andrews Golfers was formed there were 22 holes on the course, which started on the hill behind the present R & A clubhouse. In 1764 it was reduced to 18 holes, a precedent which was to be followed throughout the world as the game expanded more than a century later. The original course was also much narrower than it is today, with the sea coming right up to the edge of the first fairway, and with much larger areas of the prickly whin bushes which bear bright yellow flowers in early summer.

Perhaps the first golfing photograph ever taken, this picture shows the Union Parlour in 1848. Six years later the Union Club joined with the R & A in building the present clubhouse and the two clubs subsequently amalgamated in 1877.

This photograph, taken in the 1930s, clearly shows the problems, which persist to this day, posed by pedestrians crossing the first and eighteenth fairway of the Old Course on their way to the West Sands.

To add to the problems, the 11 outward holes were merely played in reverse order on the way home, with only one flag on each green. Homeward players always had the right-of-way over those going out, and that tradition continues to this day, although largely to discourage the often laboriously slow pace of modern play. The one exception is the final hole, where players coming down the first are given priority on the fairway it shares with the eighteenth.

Golfers today are often delayed and distracted on this part of the course by a constant stream of pedestrians crossing to the West Sands. But it was much worse in the middle of the eighteenth century when horses and carts would pass this way and local women exercised their right to lay their washing on the ground to dry. No wonder the early members of the R & A were in urgent need of a seven-course meal and eight bottles of claret at the end of a round.

Those who took that sort of punishment, both on and off the course, had to have constitutions more akin to an ox than a human. John Whyte Melville was certainly of that breed. Captain of the club in 1823, he struck a bizarre wager with Sir David Moncrieffe, the outcome of which could only be settled when one of them died, for the survivor was to present a silver putter to the club. In fact, Melville outlived his great friend by 50 years, during which time he continued to play 36 holes of golf three days a week over the Old Course, in summer and winter, until the age of 83. He died shortly before taking office as captain for the second time – 60 years after his first appointment.

For feats of strength and endurance Melville was outdone by only one other member. Captain Maitland Dougall, later to become an admiral, was getting ready to play in the Autumn Medal of 1860 when a ship was seen to be in distress in St Andrews Bay. The weather was atrocious, with gale-force winds and mountainous seas. The lifeboat was housed close to where Rusacks Hotel now stands and as it was dragged across the golf course to be launched at the mouth of the Swilcan Burn it was discovered that the crew were short of one man.

Maitland Dougall abandoned his golf clubs and volunteered to take the place of the missing man. He took the stroke oar and spent the next five hours battling the elements in a successful rescue. James Gourlay, the famous maker of featherie balls, watched the scene and described conditions as the worst he had ever seen. 'I wouldn't have set foot in that boat for a thousand pounds', he said later.

Despite the battering he had taken, Maitland Dougall was determined not to miss his golf and immediately the lifeboat was safely ashore he set out to play his round. He had earlier taken the precaution of boring a hole in his gutta ball and filling it with buckshot to keep it low in the wind. His score of 112 would suggest that it was not a wholly successful ploy, but no-one throughout that tumultuous day had done any better and he won the medal with the highest score ever.

A century later another naval member of the R & A left his permanent mark on the Old Course, where a deep bunker on the twelfth fairway has been known ever since as The Admiral. That was the rank of C.H.G. Benson when he was distracted by a very attractive female golfer on the nearby seventh. Pat Ward-Thomas, in his history, *The Royal and Ancient*, recounted that: 'Unwisely he did not avert his gaze in time to see the bunker and suddenly vanished, keel over masthead, trolley-cart, clubs and all from sight of his companions.'

LEFT *A player of 1893 stands poised for his shot, using his caddie's back to secure his footing – definitely not legal today!*

OVERLEAF *The atmosphere of traditional links golf is vividly captured in this shot of the twelfth on the Old Course.*

By 1824 it had been decided that the captaincy should not be left to the fluctuating fortunes of those who played for the silver club, but that the man to lead the members for the next year should be selected and nominated. This made it possible for the names of five royal captains to appear on the club honours boards, something which would not have been possible if decided purely by their golfing ability.

The captain-elect goes through the nerve-wracking experience of driving himself into office on the first tee of the Old Course. Led from the clubhouse by the honorary professional and accompanied by past captains and members, he waits impatiently for eight o'clock and for the professional to tee his ball.

To add to the tension a small cannon is wheeled out beside the tee and prepared for firing as soon as the new captain has struck the ball. The first such cannon was bought from a Prussian captain in 1837 for £2, but replaced with a slightly more expensive version in 1892 when it was feared that the original might take the captain's head off. Lined up across the fairway are the local caddies, for the one who retrieves the captain's ball is presented with a gold sovereign.

There will have been much studying of form before the event and a captain with an habitual slice will not feel any more confident about his shot when confronted by a line of caddies leaning on the out-of-bounds fence on the right. When the Prince of Wales, later to become the Duke of Windsor, one of the keenest golfers the royal family has ever produced, drove himself into office in 1922 it was reported that: 'The caddies stood disloyally close.' Protocol will not come between a caddie and a gold sovereign.

BELOW A new captain drives himself into office under the watchful eye of Willie Auchterlonie, the R & A professional from 1934 onwards.
INSET LEFT *The cannon salutes the incoming captain.*
INSET RIGHT. *The Prince of Wales, later King Edward VIII, captain in 1922, with Lord Castlerosse.*

ABOVE *The 'new' clubhouse and members, photographed at, or shortly after, its opening in 1854.*

During these years of increasing authority and affluence the club had moved from the back room of the tavern run by Ballie Glass to share premises overlooking the golf course with the Union Club. The present-day clubhouse, much expanded in recent years, was built jointly by the R & A and the Union Club in 1854, although the Union Club always appeared to be the partner which paid the bills, including the £50 a year salary given to Old Tom Morris when he was appointed Keeper of the Green. The two clubs were officially amalgamated in 1877 and it is the old Union Club silver which is still used in the R & A dining room.

As well as their move into a spacious new clubhouse, the R & A also moved into a position of increased responsibility within the game. When the first Open Championship belt was won outright by Young Tom Morris in 1870, the Prestwick Club, which had inaugurated the contest in 1860 and had run it for ten years, looked to St Andrews and Edinburgh for help in providing funds for a new trophy. Agreement over the amounts involved was not something to be rushed and no decision had been made in time to hold the championship in the following year. In fact, it was only a few days before the 1872 event that the three clubs involved made the crucial breakthrough and the championship was saved. Since that date only world war has interrupted the world's oldest event.

Initially the Prestwick, St Andrews and Musselburgh courses each hosted the contest once every three years; then, when the Honorable Company of Edinburgh Golfers opened their new course at Muirfield in 1892, they took the championship with them from the old nine-hole links at Musselburgh and two years later it was played on an English course for the first time. As the championship expanded and was played on a greater number of different courses a consortium of 26 golf clubs became involved in its organization.

The sheer weight of numbers made efficient administration difficult and in 1919 a unanimous decision was made to hand over the running of the Open and the Amateur Championships to the Royal and Ancient. In addition the Club is now responsible for the Boys and Youths Championships and for selecting teams for the Walker Cup and World Amateur Team Championships as well as many other international matches within Europe.

A similar situation arose with the general administration of the game and although the R & A had nothing to do with framing the original rules of golf in 1744, they had become an accepted authority 150 years later when the most powerful clubs decided that a uniform code of rules was essential. Once again the R & A was the natural choice and the first Rules of Golf Committee sat in 1897. This continues to be an important area of administration for the club. With the exception of the United States and Mexico, where the United States Golf Association is the governing body, every country in the world looks to St Andrews for guidance on the rules. The close cooperation between the R & A and the USGA has resulted in a common worldwide code for many years.

One of the most significant changes in these rules, which took place in 1951, was the abolition of the stymie. In the early days of the game, balls could not be marked and lifted on the putting green. If one ball lay in the path of another it was called a stymie and the furthest ball had to be chipped over it to reach the hole. This was considered an unfair part of the modern game and the rule rescinded. But the well-filled cellars of the R & A contain a popular whisky called 'Stymie' and many years later, when a diligent golf correspondent telephoned the R & A to enquire when the stymie had been abolished, he was assured by an earnest lady: 'It's not been abolished, sir. I can see a bottle from here.'

Such are the complexities of today's rules that some two thousand decisions are given every year by the Rules Committee and their permanent staff. Most are of the complicated 'If player A's ball hits player B and rebounds to knock player C's ball out of bounds' variety. Much easier to handle was a query from Africa. As a player reached the top of his backswing a snake slithered between his feet. With a quick adjustment to his downswing he sliced off the snake's head. Did this count as a stroke? The Rules Committee decided that in all fairness such skill should not be penalized.

Thus, from its modest beginnings in 1754 the R & A has grown and has had greatness thrust upon it. It is still a rather exclusive private club with some 1,700 members worldwide. Influential administrators and supporters from all golfing nations form a great part of this membership. Only about fifty full members actually live in St Andrews.

The organization of championships and the application of the rules is carried out by a small team of professional administrators supported by members' committees, the whole operation master-minded by a man who enjoyed great success in the amateur game, Michael Bonallack. Although he once described his own swing as being more suited to shovelling coal, he was five times the winner of the British and the English Amateur Championships and four times the English stroke-play champion. He played in the Walker Cup matches against America nine times and, quite fittingly, led the home team to victory in St Andrews in 1971.

His predecessor, the late Keith Mackenzie, was the man responsible for guiding the Open Championship into the modern era. He built up the overseas entry, increased prize money and created spectator facilities and comforts previously unknown. This was of great importance for the R & A, for it is during the Open Championship that its work comes under the closest public scrutiny. Even so, most of those who enjoy watching the golf still remain

Michael Bonallack, the Secretary of the R & A, is presented with a copy of the new edition of the Rules of Golf.

INSET *Brigadier Eric Brickman, Secretary from 1952 to 1967.*

unaware of the benefits which the multi-million pound event brings to the game as a whole. Although it takes about £1 million to put in the necessary infrastructure at the course chosen to host the championship, the worldwide interest in the event is such that it makes healthy profits. This money is carefully used to promote golf from grass-roots level, with more than £1 million being ploughed back into the game each year. The Golf Foundation scheme for junior golf coaching has been a major beneficiary and cash has also gone to students and handicapped golfers in Britain and overseas. Money has also been provided to fund a major investigation into the need for, and provision of, new courses and into green-keeping methods. Many small clubs have also received grants to help expand facilities in an ongoing effort to improve quality and find room for the next generation of golfers.

Despite having the responsibilities of the golfing world on their shoulders the administrators and members of the R & A have never lost sight of the original intentions of those 22 noblemen and gentlemen of Fife who started it all 250 years ago. Golf is still followed by good food and drink in companionable surroundings and the words of James Balfour, spoken in 1870, still have an uncanny ring of truth today.

Each golfer dilates on his own wonderful strokes and the singular chances that befell him in the different parts of the green, all under the pleasurable delusion that every listener is as interested in his game as he is.

Some things in golf never change.

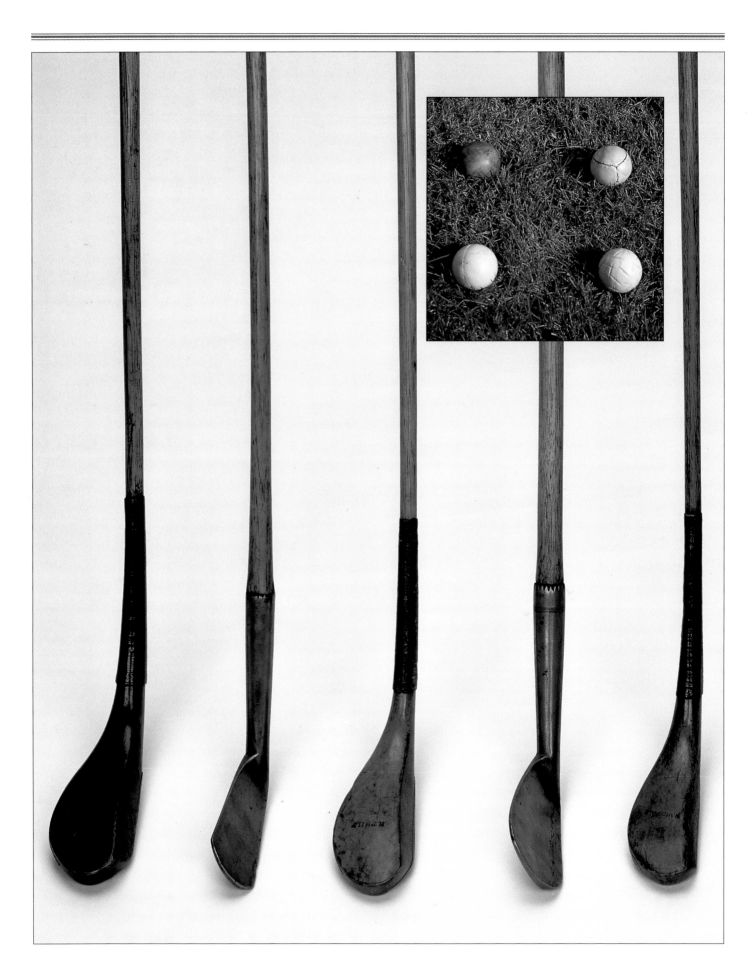

Chapter 3

HICKORY SHAFTS, FEATHERIE BALLS

ST ANDREWS HAS BEEN HOME not only to many of the game's great players, but also to whole dynasties of craftsmen who have made a significant contribution to the development of the clubs and balls which modern golfers take, perhaps too readily, for granted. For the history of golfing equipment is a long and fascinating one, and the way in which that equipment has changed over the centuries has had a dramatic effect both on the golf swing and on the design of courses.

As already noted in Chapter 1, the origins of golf are obscure and we may reasonably suppose that the first golf stroke amounted to no more than the casual swing of a stray branch at a smooth pebble. But once something resembling a recognized game began to emerge there was a demand for purpose-built equipment which would give a player an edge over his rivals. Soon, roughly shaped wooden balls replaced stones and the help of experienced bowyers was enlisted to splice wooden heads and shafts together and thus create the first custom-built clubs.

The early clubmakers used a method called scaring which had been perfected by boat-builders for making masts. The head and shaped neck of the club were worked from a single piece of wood and a deep V-shaped cut made in the neck. The shaft was tapered to an exact fit and the two glued together. Rope strands were unravelled, dipped in pitch and bound tightly around the joint for extra strength and to keep the union water-tight.

The accounts of the Lord High Treasurer of Scotland dated February 1503, in the reign of James IV, contain the earliest recorded mention of the purchase of golf equipment, an entry which notes the purchase of 'golf clubbes and ballis to the King'. A century later the game was well enough established for the court to require the services of a royal clubmaker.

The first description of the clubs in common use in those early days comes from Thomas Kincaid who noted, in 1687, that they had 'shafts of hazel which should be long and supple with the head at a very obtuse angle to the shaft.' Clubs matching that design were still the major weapons in the game two centuries later, although by this time hazel and ash shafts had been superseded by American hickory, which came into use from about 1825.

A selection of hickory-shafted clubs. The heads of the wooden clubs were spliced onto the shafts and the splice was then bound with tarred twine. In the case of the irons, the shaft is fitted into a socket in the neck of the club-head.
INSET *Four early golf balls; a wooden ball, in use up to the sixteenth century, a featherie, and two examples of gutta percha balls from the nineteenth century.*

Strong and straight-grained, hickory was the perfect wood for golf shafts, surviving for a century, well into the age of mass production, before steel finally took over in the 1920s. These wooden shafts were lovingly created by craftsmen. They had to be shaped and smoothed out of the rough timber and then finely tapered towards the clubhead. Finally the wood was shaved and scraped to produce a helpful kick or spring in exactly the right spot when the head impacted with the ball. A master clubmaker could match one shaft with another by eye and feel.

Club-heads were fashioned from a variety of woods. At first beech, apple or blackthorn was used, but again it was a very dense American hardwood which finally came to dominate all other materials. Persimmon-headed clubs hit the ball further and lasted longer. Even today, when metal woods – a typically modern contradiction in terms – have swept the popular market, persimmon drivers are much prized by many professionals.

Early club-heads were long and slender, with little depth or width. They were virtually man-made replicas of the natural, gently curved tree limbs which had been the first clubs. With such long-shafted, slender equipment the ideal swing was one which swept the ball off the turf, brushing the grass but not gouging deep divots. Heavy contact with the ground could snap the rather fragile shafts, and this was obviously a common occurrence. The rules of golf, committed to paper for the first time in 1744, made two references to broken clubs. Golfers were not allowed to pick up the pieces if shattered shafts interfered with the lie of the ball, and if a club snapped after the downswing had begun it was to be counted as a stroke.

The accepted style of play was to adopt a wide stance, with the left foot drawn well back in what would today be described as an open position. Because the early golfers were trying to sweep the ball away, rather than hitting down and through in modern style, the plane of the swing was relatively flat. This meant that the club was swung round the back of the shoulders rather than above the head.

No attention was paid to a straight left arm or a steady head position. Anything which encouraged a long, flowing swing was acceptable. There was also a pronounced movement into and through the ball with the upper body, many of the leading players almost throwing themselves off balance. Young Tom Morris, the best player of his era, was often reported to have dislodged his cap with the force of his shots as he swayed violently into the ball.

The shape of clubs and the consequent inelegance of swing style might well have lasted to this day if there had not been fundamental changes to the golf ball.

By the early 1600s Scots golfers had exchanged the solid wooden ball for something altogether more amenable – the featherie. The Romans had used a similar ball for the game they called *paganica*, but whether some seventeenth-century golfer had found a reference to the earlier ball, or whether it was reinvented, there is no way of knowing. The name came simply from the goose feathers which were the ball's stuffing. Manufacture was long and laborious and even the best workers could make no more than six in a full day. The average was only four.

Three pieces of leather were shaped, soaked in alum water, stitched together and then turned inside out, leaving a small hole through which to insert the feathers. Tradition has it that a top hat full of feathers was required for every ball. In reality it was probably twice that amount. They were boiled to reduce their bulk and painstakingly inserted into the small leather cover. As the job neared completion the task became more and more difficult. The great pressure required to get the last of the feathers into the ball was usually achieved by placing a cross-handled rod against the chest. Then the hole was stitched up and the ball left to dry.

As the leather shrank the drying feathers expanded and these opposing pressures produced a ball that was firm and solid, yet with a certain amount of resilience. But it was not very durable, often opening up at the seams in the wet, and easily cut. It was also expensive, costing as much as a new club. Yet despite the drawbacks it served the golfers of St Andrews and the rest of Scotland well for some 250 years.

The next advance in the manufacture of the golf ball was to have even more far-reaching effects than the switch from wood to feathers. Gutta percha, a hard rubbery tree sap which was imported into Britain from the mid-1840s, could be easily moulded when boiled. The first guttie balls, as they quickly became known, were hand-rolled and far from perfect, but they were cheap and almost indestructible. And if they did become badly marked they could simply be heated and remoulded.

BELOW LEFT *Early gutta and featherie balls.*
RIGHT *A close-up of a featherie made in about 1845. The seams in the leather casing are clearly visible.*

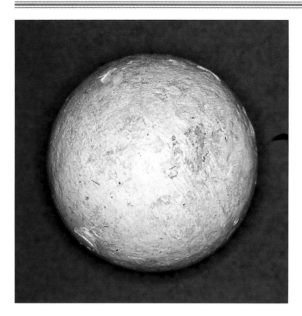

The first of these new balls may have been made by a St Andrews clergyman, the Rev Dr R. Paterson. A well known, but unsubstantiated, local story tells how he received a present of a small Hindu statue from a friend in the Far East. Inside its box it was protected by lumps of hard, rubbery material which he heated and converted into a golf ball in April 1845. Golfing experts give no credence to the tale, but intriguingly a small Hindu statue survives in a museum in Dundee – presented by a Rev James Paterson.

There is, in fact, no hard evidence to show who made the first guttie ball, but its popularity spread like wildfire, bringing the game back within the reach of those who could not afford the featheries and only played when they were lucky enough to find them in the thick whin bushes which bordered the Old Course and most other Scottish links. Iron and brass moulds were soon produced which could quickly turn a lump of raw gutta percha into a round, smooth golf ball. But at first the results were disappointing, for in its perfect state the smooth ball dipped quickly into the ground; only after a little harsh treatment did it begin to fly correctly. Without understanding the aerodynamics, makers would chisel or hammer patterns into the new, solid balls, achieving greater and greater success in terms of flight and distance. Soon they were producing moulds with built-in patterns – some with raised pimples, others with sunken dimples.

The new balls sold in their hundreds, threatening the livelihood of those who had specialized in the production of featheries. Allan Robertson, recognized as the first professional golfer and the greatest player of his day, paid St Andrews schoolboys to bring him any of the new balls they found on the course so that he could burn them and turn back the tide of progress to save his own featherie business. It was a forlorn gesture.

What no-one realized, in the first enthusiastic rush to use the new ball, was that it would lead to massive changes in the design of clubs and ultimately alter the shape of the golf swing. The simple truth was that the long-nosed, elegant wooden clubs of the featherie era were just not strong enough to cope with the solid guttie ball. Dents and cracks began to appear in the well-crafted clubs and modifications were necessary. At first strips of leather were inserted into the club-face to lessen the impact, but these quickly wore out and were replaced with horn. A further problem was that there was not sufficient substance in the narrow heads to cope with the heavier ball. A solution was to add extra lead into hollows in the back of the club, but the long shafts – 45 inches on average – made control difficult. A more radical rethink was needed, and by 1880 new clubs were in use with shorter shafts, reduced by three inches to 42 inches, and the angle between shaft and head had become slightly more upright. At the same time, the heads of wooden clubs had become shorter, but much deeper and broader, with a greater concentration of weight, and had solid face inserts to prevent damage.

There were also changes made to the profile of the faces of the wooden clubs, which had traditionally been given a concave shape. The new style featured a convex face which led to the clubs being known as 'bulgers'. The initial intention was to concentrate the weight in the centre of the face, but it was soon discovered that the 'bulgers' had the additional advantage of minimizing hook and slice spin.

The switch to the guttie ball also drastically reduced the number of wooden clubs in use. A typical set in the featherie era would have contained perhaps eight or ten assorted woods, from the play club, or driver, through to a variety of spoons and baffing spoons, plus a wooden niblick and putter. There would have been only two iron clubs, used for extracting the ball from cart ruts and bunkers. For iron club-heads and featherie balls did not go well together – a single ill-judged shot could slice through the cover and destroy the ball.

But iron clubs could do little to damage the tough, new ball and they were easier and cheaper to make than wooden clubs. Heads were hand-forged with a hollow socket into which the tapered wooden shafts were fitted. Early iron clubs had smooth faces, but by 1900 the fashion of cutting grooves or punching indentations into the metal was giving a noticeable amount of backspin and greater control over the flight of the ball.

The second half of the nineteenth century and the early part of the twentieth saw an incredible growth in the popularity of the game. In 1864 there were no more than thirty golf clubs in Scotland – and just three across the border in England. By 1891 the total number in Britain had grown to 481; by 1900 it had mushroomed to 1,571; and by 1909 it had virtually doubled to 2,786.

The gutta ball and iron club-heads made mass production of golf equipment possible, and very necessary. American hickory had swept the board and was the number-one choice for all golf shafts. The demand was enormous. On one occasion A.G. Spalding & Bros, with offices in London's Fetter Lane and a factory at Putney Wharf, advertised the importation of a quarter of a million 'second-growth hickory shafts in splendid condition' which they offered to club manufacturers, with discounts of up to 20 per cent on orders for ten thousand shafts.

Gutta balls were promoted in glowing terms. Hunter's Special called on champions John Ball and Harold Hilton to endorse their product – 'He never played with a better' and 'They fly well and keep exceptionally true' were typical of the quotes used in their advertisements. But the dominance of the new, miracle ball was to be relatively short; it would endure barely half a century compared with the 250-year reign of the featherie.

It was just before the turn of the century that a wealthy American amateur golfer named Coburn Haskell developed his idea for a more resilient golf ball, with assistance from Bertram Work, then an engineer with the Goodrich Rubber Company in Akron, Ohio. Haskell reasoned that by introducing a rubber core into the gutta ball he could give it more bounce and enable golfers to hit greater distances. In order to give the ball the sort of initial velocity he was seeking it was necessary to wind enormous lengths of rubber thread into a core under pressure. Early prototypes lacked stability and tended to veer off line or to duck into the ground. Only when an automatic winding machine was developed were Haskell's attempts successful.

ABOVE *A niblick made in the early years of this century. Note the indentations in the club-face, a development that came into fashion around 1900.*
INSET *An iron of about the same period. Both club-heads are hand-forged.*

Coburn Haskell, the American inventor of the wound rubber core which still forms the heart of the modern golf ball. Appropriately enough, he is pictured holding a branch from a rubber plant.

The new balls were a revelation. Good players were gaining 30 yards and more from the tee, although the lively feel off the club-face initially caused them problems of control around the green. Commercial production started in America in 1901 and, in essence, that product is the ball still in use around the world today.

Haskell's invention quickly produced a crop of imitations and warning notices soon appeared in newspapers and golf clubs alerting golfers to the fact that the sale of

> foreign-made golf balls having centres made of rubber under tension is an infringement of the Haskell United States patent. Dealers and players handling or using such balls render themselves liable to legal proceedings.

One of the first converts to the new ball was Sandy Herd, a canny Scot who thought it worth paying almost eight times the normal price to get his hands on one of them just before the Open Championship of 1902 at Hoylake. He quickly adjusted to the totally different feel of the Haskell and beat Harry Vardon and James Braid to the title by one stroke, although the ball was in decidedly poor shape by the finish – parts of its wound rubber interior being clearly visible.

Ironically, the Home of Golf might have laid claim to the fame, and the financial rewards, that in the event went to Coburn Haskell. For a St Andrews player had produced a small number of wound rubber balls some thirty years before Haskell embarked on his venture. Duncan Stewart, a retired naval captain, made a hobby of experimenting with golf balls, amusing his friends with guttie balls to which he had added iron filings or cork, and one of his ideas, which went down quite well with his golfing partners, was a ball which featured lengths of rubber thread inside the gutta percha. But Stewart felt no inclination to persevere with the idea, and by the time Haskell started his experiments in America he had moved away from St Andrews and given up the game.

Since that time the basic construction of the ball has remained the same, although there have been tremendous advances in materials and aerodynamic technology which have led to much greater control and lower scoring.

It was to be almost another thirty years before golf clubs broke completely free from the shackles of the past and wooden shafts were left behind as clubmakers moved into the age of steel.

Initially there were difficulties in manufacturing tubular steel shafts which were strong but both light and flexible. By 1929, however, the problems had been solved, and in that year the Royal and Ancient determined that steel shafts came within the accepted limits of the rules which governed the form and make of clubs.

Although many traditionalists mourned the passing of the hickory age, the advent of steel made it possible to mass-produce matched sets of clubs. The master craftsmen who spent painstaking hours in shaving and whittling wooden shafts to achieve some semblance of compatibility between one club and the next were replaced by machines, which could spew out thousands of identical shafts each week, all of a specific size, shape, flex, and weight.

The new shafts were also much stronger, a factor which led to a revolution in the golf swing, transforming the flat, sweeping action of the past into the upright power method of today. A move in this direction had already been started by Harry Vardon, who remains the only man to have won the Open Championship six times. Together with J.H. Taylor and James Braid he dominated the game for two decades, starting his winning run in 1896 and capturing his final title in 1914. He broke away from the very flat swing which had always been the accepted style of play and picked the club up much more steeply in the backswing. He turned his shoulders and hips a full 90 degrees so that, at the top of his swing, his back was facing the hole. There was a pronounced bend in his left arm and a tendency for the right elbow to fly away from the body, but this method allowed him to hit the ball much higher than his contemporaries in an age when low trajectory running shots were still the accepted way to play the game.

A selection of the mass-produced, steel-shafted clubs which rapidly supplanted the old wooden-shafted, hand-made clubs from 1929 onwards.

Worth considering!

1910

A Happy and Successful New Year is ensured to Golfers
by playing the

Dunlop Ball.

This is guaranteed by the splendid record of Championships and big events
during the past season. Start the New Year well, your professional will give you
the opportunity of trying the "Orange Spot" or "Junior." By-the-bye, a box of
Dunlops makes a nice and highly appreciated New Year's Gift. Supplied in boxes
containing 2, 3, 4, 6, or 1 dozen.

Prices: "Orange Spot" 2/- each; "Junior" 2/- each; Manor Ball 1/3 each.
If unable to obtain a supply locally, write us direct:
DUNLOP RUBBER CO., LTD., Manor Mills, Aston, BIRMINGHAM.

TEE YOUR BALL ON CONFIDENCE
IN THIS NAME

The
REDDY
TEE

THE TEE OF CHAMPIONS
...because they demand the
finest in EVERY item of their
golfing equipment...because
the REDDY TEE was the FIRST tee
they ever used and because
their confidence in the original
golf tee of the world has never
wavered.

"BUY FROM YOUR PRO"

The Nieblo Mfg. Co., Inc.   38 East 23rd Street
New York, N.Y.

TOP LEFT *By 1910, when this
advertisement appeared, the
wound rubber ball had swept the
board with golfers on both sides
of the Atlantic.*

TOP RIGHT *An
advertisement for one of the
new brands of tee which came
into use in the 1930s.*

LEFT *Tom Auchterlonie's shop,
part of a long tradition of
clubmaking in St Andrews.*

OPPOSITE *The Tom Morris
shop beside the eighteenth
fairway.*

RIGHT *Robert Forgan, a celebrated St Andrews clubmaker around the turn of the century, in his workshop.*
BELOW *The various stages in the production of a modern golf ball.*

CENTRE BALLOON

CENTRE BALLOON FILLED

HAND-BINDING TAPE

CENTRE HAND BOUND

MACHINE WINDING TAPE

CORE MACHINE WOUND

RUBBER THREAD

CENTRE RUBBER THREAD WOUND

HALF SECTION COVERS

HALF SECTION COVERS FITTED

BALL MOULDED

MOULDED BALL TRIMMED

NUMERALS PAINTED IN

NUMERALS CLEANED, LETTERING PAINTED IN

FINISHED BALL

WRAPPED BALL

This more upright, straight-line swing gave Vardon legendary accuracy and he was renowned for fading fairway woods close to the hole. Yet the restrictions imposed by the lack of strength in wooden shafts caused him to sweep the ball off the grass, just shaving the turf, rather than taking divots in the modern manner.

The introduction of steel shafts changed all that – much to the aggravation of green-keepers everywhere. The stronger clubs allowed players to hit down firmly into the back of the ball, an action which generates maximum backspin. This gets the ball airborne more quickly and holds it on line. It also makes it possible to bring the ball to a controlled stop with shots into the green.

The development of the wound ball and steel shafts were giant steps in the evolution of the game and, despite the massive funds devoted to research by modern equipment manufac-turers, no equivalent quantum leaps in golfing technology are currently in prospect. Instead there has been a constant programme of improvement, particularly in the design and manu-facture of the ball. While leading tournament professionals gain incredible control over wound balls with thin balata covers, the majority of the world's golfers now get added dis-tance and cut-proof durability from a ball made from a solid resin core with a surlyn cover.

Advances in club design have been spearheaded by the development of peripheral weight-ing, where the mass of the club-head is concentrated around the periphery of the face, a process which creates a much larger hitting area. Shafts are now made in ever increasing numbers from carbon-fibre and graphite, materials much lighter than steel but just as strong. Wooden heads are similarly giving way to hollow metal blocks, carbon, graphite, and even ceramics.

The production of equipment which allows the average golfer to hit the ball further, and with greater control, has encouraged course designers to set new challenges, while many older courses have been lengthened to cope with the changes.

When our golfing ancestors were tackling the Old Course with wooden clubs and feath-erie or guttie balls they would sweep the shots away with a low, running trajectory, walking a tightrope between bunkers and whins as they tried to thread the ball through towards the green. Today's Open Champions smash their wind-tunnel-tested balata missiles high into the air with graphite-shafted, peripheral-weighted irons and make them screw to a stop on the hardest of greens as if under remote control.

It is the same game – but it is also very different.

Chapter 4

1873–1910

OPEN CHAMPIONSHIPS I

SINCE THE OPEN CHAMPIONSHIP was first played at Prestwick in 1860 only war has prevented the annual playing of the oldest of golf's major contests – except for 1871, when no trophy was available. The problem arose because Young Tom Morris had walked away with the original one the previous year. There was nothing remotely illegal in his actions. He had merely proved that he was the finest golfer of his time by winning the championship three years in a row – and by increasingly large margins. According to the custom of the day his third successive victory gave him the outright possession of the trophy, a handsome, wide belt of red Moroccan leather intricately worked with silver. It had cost 25 guineas when members of the Prestwick club first came up with the idea for a championship and invited leading clubs to send 'known and respectable caddies' to compete.

In 1868 Young Tom beat his father by three shots, the following year he left the field 11 shots in his wake, and in 1870 he increased that winning margin to 12 strokes over 36 holes. These were incredibly low scores – his total of 149 for three rounds of the 12-hole course in 1870 was equivalent to 18-hole scores of 74 and 75. They clearly left Prestwick members in a state of shock and, more seriously, without a trophy.

The Prestwick club appealed to their contemporaries at Edinburgh and St Andrews for help, help which was not forthcoming in time for the 1871 contest to take place. In fact, the joint decision by Prestwick Golf Club, the Honourable Company of Edinburgh Golfers and the Royal and Ancient to put up money for a trophy and thus resurrect the Championship after a year in abeyance, was so long delayed that the new trophy was not ready for the 1872 event. Research through the records of the Prestwick Club and the R & A show that it was only two days before 13 September, the scheduled date of the Championship, that final agreement was reached on how the cost of a new trophy should be split.

As a stop-gap measure a medal bearing the same inscription – 'Golf Champion Trophy' – was presented to the winner, Young Tom yet again; but it was to be another year before his name was engraved on the new trophy, an exquisite claret jug, and he was able to

Young Tom Morris wearing the belt which was the original Open Championship trophy. He won the belt outright with his third Championship victory in 1870.

handle it for the first, and last, time. Nor was his 1872 medal quite the real thing, being gold-plated base metal, unlike those presented later, which were solid gold.

Today the original trophy is normally kept in the R & A clubhouse and the one carried away by the new champion each year is, in reality, an early replica, made just a few years after 1873. But Tom Watson once got away with the real thing, returning it at the following year's championship with apologies for a small dent he had caused in the precious jug. The R & A's silver expert, John Bowles, discovered the mistake when he was called in to advise on repairs. Following their success in gaining financial support from Edinburgh and the R & A, Prestwick then asked for the help of the other two clubs in staging the annual contest, and from 1873 on it was agreed that it should be played at each of the three locations in turn.

Because of its isolated position, Prestwick had never attracted large entries. The majority of Scotland's courses were on the east coast and it was a lengthy and expensive round trip to the western side of the country for one day's play, even if it was to decide the champion golfer. In singularly pragmatic fashion, players would stay at home if there was no realistic chance of winning. On one occasion four local amateurs had been drafted into the field at the last moment to make the numbers up to eight.

When the Championship finally came to St Andrews for the first time in 1873 there were many more players and a local victory, but also an overall sense of anticlimax. After the low-scoring exploits of Young Tom Morris, the standard of play drew disparaging remarks in contemporary accounts of the event and when local caddie Tom Kidd could win with rounds of 91 and 88 over the 18-hole course it is easy to see why experts felt the quality of play was far below average. Newspaper reports spoke eloquently of the perfect conditions for the 36 holes played on 4 October that year, with bright sun and no wind to disturb the flight of the gutta balls. But there were also fleeting mentions of pools of water on the course after heavy rain earlier in the week. Obviously the holes would have been playing to their full length in these conditions and it is possible that the leading contenders fell foul of the puddles, for there were no free drops from casual water in those days and each excursion into the hidden pools would have cost a stroke.

Certainly, for Young Tom Morris, the defending champion, to return scores of 94 and 89 for third place there must have been extenuating circumstances. He had, after all, lowered the Old Course record to 77 shots the previous year. Undoubtedly the greatest golfer of his day, he was destined never to win at St Andrews – by the time the Championship returned in 1876 he had died at the age of 24.

If 1873 was a high-scoring anticlimax, the Championship of 1876 was more a comedy of errors. Members of the R & A were determined to play their own golf despite the need to complete the 36-hole Championship. The 34 official entrants in the Open took alternate start times on the first tee with local golfers – and the result was chaos. There were lengthy delays around the course and many cases of players hitting into the match in front. What drama there was centred on David Strath, a St Andrean who had been appointed professional at North Berwick. Strath felled a local golfer with a full-blooded shot at the fourteenth on the crowded links; it gave the victim a severe lump on the head and cost Strath a six. When he arrived at the seventeenth he needed to finish with two fives to beat the not very impressive target of 176 set by Bob Martin. His third shot to the dangerous par four rattled into the players ahead while they were still putting, but he safely got down in two. Then a poor six at the last tied Martin's score and a play-off was set for the following Monday.

But Strath's play at the seventeenth had drawn a complaint and a demand that he be disqualified. The R & A, unbelievably, decided to defer a decision on his disqualification until after the play-off, but Strath refused to play until a ruling had been given. As small and unyielding as the bunker at the eleventh green that bears his name, Strath stood behind the first tee on that fateful Monday morning and learned that the governing officials of the R & A would not relent. He watched in embittered silence as Bob Martin set off to walk round the course and claim the title.

INSET *Bob Martin, who won the claret jug in 1876 after the debacle caused by an overcrowded Old Course and a bizarre decision by the R & A.*

LEFT *David Strath, who lost the 1876 Championship after refusing to take part in a play-off against Bob Martin.*

It was yet another St Andrean who triumphed over the largest entry ever received for the Championship when 46 players arrived in the old grey city in 1879. Jamie Anderson was under pressure from the start, having won the title in the two previous years. He was eager to become a triple champion and carried all the hopes and expectations of the home crowd. His long face, hooded eyes, swept-back hair and small beard gave him an almost aristocratic look which belied his poor background. His father was a caddie and he had learned the game from an early age. His rather languid appearance and his uncanny ability to walk straight up to the ball and play a perfect shot with almost nonchalant speed were allied to a devastating short game. When playing for his first championship at Prestwick a 4,4,3,4 finish would have tied him for the title. But he pitched into the hole at the fifteenth and holed in one at the seventeenth to win by two clear shots.

There were to be no such heroics at St Andrews, where once again the scoring was high. Prestwick-born Jamie Allan was Anderson's closest contender, closing the gap between their scores to only one shot after nine holes of the second round, but over the closing holes Anderson's steadiness under pressure eventually gave him a comfortable three-stroke margin for his third consecutive victory.

BELOW LEFT Jamie Anderson in 1867; twelve years later, at St Andrews, he was to gain his third Open title.
BELOW RIGHT A group portrait painted in 1905 showing the Open Champions of the day.

One of the new generation of St Andrews golfers, 19-year-old Andrew Kirkaldy, joined Allan in second place with two rounds of 86. The young Kirkaldy was destined for a glittering career, but never the title of Champion Golfer.

Anderson's opportunity to match Young Tom Morris' feat in winning four consecutive Open Championships was lost when notification of the following year's event at Musselburgh reached him too late and he was not in the field; but he did finish second and third in the next two years.

FAR LEFT *Bob Ferguson, a three-time winner of the Open who triumphed at St Andrews in 1882.* LEFT *Willie Fernie, runner-up to Ferguson in 1882. He gained his revenge the following year at Musselburgh, denying Ferguson his fourth title.*

The man who took over the mantle of champion from Jamie Anderson was also destined to win three times in a row. Bob Ferguson started his run of success over his home course of Musselburgh and beat Anderson into second place the following year at Prestwick. None of the early St Andrews Opens were marked by low scoring and the Championship of 1882 was no exception. Ferguson's opening round of 83 was three shots clear of any other contender and although he could manage no better than an 88 in the afternoon he was a convincing winner over Willie Fernie, yet another St Andrean, who was then professional at Dumfries. By one of those ironic twists of fate, Fernie was to rob Ferguson of his fourth title by beating him in a play-off at Musselburgh the following year.

Rewards for Open Championship success in those days were slim, a few pounds at most, and once his glory days at the top of the game were over Ferguson returned, as did most other former title-holders, to caddying and green-keeping.

Bob Martin, who had won the 1876 title when David Strath refused to take part in a play-off, repeated his St Andrews victory in 1885 as a result of 'his strong and steady game, not characterised as brilliant', in the words of one newspaper correspondent. In difficult conditions, with a cold wind from the north-west causing many problems on the outward nine holes, the foundations of his victory were laid with a score of 41 to the turn in the opening round. Two of the famous Simpson brothers from Earlsferry in Fife came close to victory, Archie finishing in second place and Bob two shots further back. Brother Jack had won the title the previous year.

ABOVE LEFT *Ben Sayers, photographed in 1911, 23 years after he narrowly lost the 1888 Open to John Burns when an error was discovered on Burns' scorecard.*
RIGHT *Ben Sayers, on left, and Archie Simpson. The caddie is 'Big' Crawford.*

A triple tie for the title when the three-club rota brought the Championship back to St Andrews in 1888 was not decided in the normal way by a 36-hole play-off, but by the sharp eye of an R & A member who spotted a scorecard error. Davie Anderson and John Burns of St Andrews were tied on 172 with Ben Sayers from North Berwick, but it was discovered that Burns' morning score of 87 had been wrongly totalled and should have been an 86. There was no question of Burns having to accept the score which had first been recorded and he was declared the champion.

Many years later at Augusta National, Open Champion Roberto de Vicenzo signed his score card on which a par four had been entered for the seventeenth hole when, in fact, he had holed a putt for a birdie three. He was forced to accept the higher score – and lost the Masters title by one shot. How he must have longed for the more simplistic days of the previous century.

But the incident in 1888 drew criticism from the *Golfing Annual*. 'Such a mistake clearly demonstrates that in future arrangements should be made by which the cards should be collected and checked by some responsible person,' they trumpeted. The same report says that Old Tom Morris, acting as starter, 'Superintended the despatch of the various couples and afterwards took part in the competition himself.' The event was played in a half-gale and Old Tom was then 67 years old.

The Championship of 1891 was significant in two ways. An entry of 82 was the largest ever assembled to decide the champion golfer and almost double any numbers that had previously competed at either Prestwick or Musselburgh, and it was to be the last title decided over 36 holes. In the following year, when Muirfield made its first appearance on the Championship scene, the 72-hole format was established. Played on 6 October, when daylight hours in St Andrews are limited, the large field nevertheless managed to complete two rounds in a single day. Play started at 9.00 in the morning and anyone not on the tee at his appointed time did not suffer today's penalties of strokes added and eventual disqualification – his name was simply placed at the bottom of the list.

The quickness of the rounds in those days would gladden the hearts of campaigners against the creeping paralysis that currently afflicts the game. A field of that same size in the 1990s would take almost seven hours to leave the first tee and the last players would be lucky to finish in daylight – and that for one round, not two.

The Championship became a family affair with Andrew Kirkaldy being accused by some locals of allowing his younger brother Hugh to win because of his increasing ill-health. But Andrew denied the charge and insisted that his 5,6 finish was the result of bad play despite his hardest efforts; and it certainly seems extremely unlikely that he would have taken chances by losing shots on the closing holes with one of the pre-tournament favourites, Willie Fernie, playing behind him. Fernie could have overtaken both Andrew and his brother, but finished in a tie for second with the older Kirkaldy. He lost the play-off for that position and the two local brothers dominated the Championship. Hugh's two rounds of 83 were in fact not very noteworthy, for the powerful golfer had previously lowered the Old Course record to 74. He was to survive only a few more years while his older brother lived to the age of 74.

*LEFT Hugh Kirkaldy, Open Champion in 1891, ponders a tricky shot followed (*BELOW*) by an even trickier one.* INSET *Andrew, Hugh's elder brother, four times runner-up for the Open Championship and Old Tom Morris' successor as the R & A professional.*

WM PARK SEN. O.C. 1860-63-66

OLD TOM MORRIS O.C. 1861-62-64 & 67

A. STRATH O.C. 1865

YOUNG TOM MORRIS O.C. 1868-69-70

JAMES BRAID O.C. 1901-5-6-8 & 10

THE JUBILEE OF THE GOLFING CHAMPIONS
·1860~1910·

BOB FERGUSON O.C. 1880-81 & 82

WILLIE FERNIE O.C. 1883

JACK SIMPSON O.C. 1884

BOB MARTIN O.C. 1876 & 1885

Harry Vardon

THE GREAT TRIUMVIRATE

The GOLFING DIPLOMA

Presented to
Score
Date
Golf Club

Hon. Sec.

DAVID BROWN O.C. 1886

WILLIE PARK JUNR. O.C. 1887-1889 & 1888

JACK BURNS O.C. 1888

MR JOHN BALL O.C. 1890

A 'Golfing Diploma' produced
to celebrate half a century of
Open Championships. It depicts
all the past champions, with
pride of place going to the 'Great
Triumvirate' of Harry Vardon,
James Braid and J.H.Taylor,
who, between them, won sixteen
Championships in 20 years.

The Open had been taken to foreign parts before next it was played at St Andrews. Royal St George's, on the Kent coast at Sandwich, was the first English venue, chosen for the Championship of 1894. The winner that year was West Country golfer J.H. Taylor, who was later to become the prime mover and founding father of the Professional Golfers' Association. He was also to form – with Harry Vardon and James Braid – the virtually unbeatable trio known in the grandiose language of Victorian Britain as the 'Great Triumvirate'. Between them they dominated the championship, capturing sixteen titles in twenty years.

It had not been expected that Taylor could repeat his success at St Andrews, for that required him to sustain his form over four rounds on bone-hard links he had never played before. Yet as the Championship progressed and the weather deteriorated with strong east winds and driving rain – despite a switch from October to June – Taylor's game improved. After a poor opening round of 86 he came back into contention with a 78, a score he repeated in the final gale-lashed round to defeat Sandy Herd by three clear shots. Andrew Kirkaldy, the strong man of St Andrews golf, was a distant third, ten strokes behind Taylor. Contemporary accounts report that the home crowds, always eager for a Scottish victory, were so impressed with Taylor's spell-binding golf that they carried the Englishman shoulder-high from the final green.

By 1900 another English course, that of the Royal Liverpool Club at Hoylake, had been added to the list of Open Championship venues and the familiar three-year cycle of championships at St Andrews was now stretched to five. But in one sense nothing had changed when the game's greatest players gathered again on the Old Course. J.H. Taylor (his initials rather than his forenames John Henry were almost invariably used throughout his career) captured his third title, stopping a run of three by Harry Vardon, just as Vardon had forestalled his hat-trick at Muirfield four years earlier.

Taylor's golf was unbeatable. He had rounds of 79,77,78,75 – the first time that 80 had been broken in every round during a St Andrews Championship. That feat had not even been accomplished when the event was played over only two rounds.

Using the solid gutta ball it was seldom that a player could carry the Swilcan Burn with his second shot to the opening hole and a long third shot was required to reach the seventeenth green. Given those restrictions Taylor's final round of 75 represented golf of outstanding quality. No wonder he left Harry Vardon eight shots adrift, with James Braid a further five shots behind in third place.

By the time the Open of 1905 was played at the Home of Golf the gutta ball had been superseded by the wound rubber ball patented in America by Coburn Haskell. The more lively ball, which added some thirty yards to the tee shots of the better players, should have made low scoring inevitable, but the weather had an important part to play, as it so often has in St Andrews. With an entry of 152 players the event was now spread over three days, one round each day on Wednesday and Thursday, with 36 holes on the Friday. A strong, cold wind from the north-east and extremely hard greens sent scores rocketing.

James Braid from nearby Earlsferry, winner of the 1901 Championship at Muirfield, had been experimenting with different clubs and discovered that on fast greens he was getting better results with an aluminium-headed putter for the long approach putts, reverting to his normal club from short range. Despite being bunkered all over the course he still managed an 81 and joint second place after the opening round. He followed with a 78 which featured a marvellous inward half of 38. He then reversed these scores for a total of 318 and victory by five shots. But his score was nine shots worse with the new ball than Taylor had managed with the old gutta five years before, although two excursions onto the railway line in the final round would not have helped. At that time the line was not out of bounds and players would hop over the fence and play recovery shots between trains. Thankfully, it was never a busy line.

BELOW *James Braid driving off the first tee at St Andrews in 1910 on the way to his fifth Open title.*
INSET *Harry Vardon, generally considered to be the 'father' of the modern swing.*

Fittingly Braid's fifth and final Championship win was accomplished at St Andrews in 1910. He was in the middle of the first round when a tremendous storm flooded many of the greens. Indecision by the governing committee left players literally floundering on the course. While some players tried to float the ball across the puddles so that it sank into the holes, others tried to chip in. One player had six putts at the second. Finally it was agreed that the course was unplayable and the round was cancelled. By this time Braid was at the thirteenth and he chose to complete the round rather than take any chances. His fine 76 was nevertheless wiped out.

Undaunted, he repeated the score the following day and added three more rounds in the seventies for a final score of 299, overtaking Sandy Herd and George Duncan for a clear victory.

Two men set a new record for the Old Course during the Championship. Both Willie Smith and George Duncan scored 71. Smith was a member of a large golfing family from Carnoustie who had settled in America. Duncan was the quicksilver Scot who once remarked of a slow opponent who was having putting problems: 'If you're going to miss them, miss them quick.' Smith followed his record score with an 80, Duncan with 83. Even then, the Old Course had a way of fighting back.

It was to be eleven years – the other side of the First World War – before Open Championship golf was to return to St Andrews.

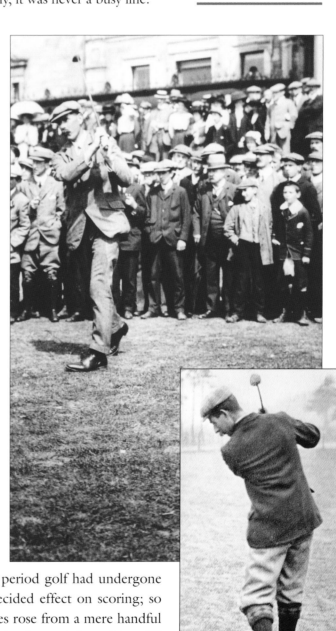

Over the course of nine Championships during a 37-year period golf had undergone many changes. The introduction of the wound ball had a decided effect on scoring; so did the change from a 4-inch hole to one of 4¼ inches. Entries rose from a mere handful of players to more than 150. The format of the Championship changed from 36 to 72 holes and the event was extended from one to three days.

Yet there were even more dramatic and far-reaching changes lurking in the not too distant future.

Chapter 5   1921–1957

OPEN CHAMPIONSHIPS II

T HE RETURN OF THE Open Championship to St Andrews in 1921 was significant for a variety of reasons: it was won for the first time by a non-British golfer (although he had been born and brought up in St Andrews); the new champion used a club which was banned a few days later; and the greatest player of the age failed to complete his first Championship over the Old Course.

Jock Hutchison had become an American citizen by the time he returned to his native St Andrews as favourite to win the title. He was armed with a special short iron with a heavily ribbed face with which he generated enormous amounts of backspin, even on the bone-hard greens that were more common in that era. He had the ability to pitch the ball past the hole and spin it back, much in the way today's professionals play the approach shots with advanced club design and far superior ball construction.

Yet a decision had already been taken by the Rules Committee of the Royal and Ancient that the type of club used by Hutchison did not comply with the form and make of golf clubs as set out in the rules. They announced that as from 1 July 1921 these clubs would be considered illegal. Jock Hutchison won his title on 25 June – just five days before the deadline. But it was not only his short game that clinched the Championship. Paired with America's outstanding young amateur, Bobby Jones, in the first round he holed in one at the eighth and nearly did so again at the next. Jones' constant companion, the gifted sports writer O.B. Keeler, described the shot:

> Jock smacked a huge drive, with a beautiful draw down a quartering wind, clear on to the ninth green, a wallop of 303 yards, the ball touching the rim of the cup and stopping three inches away for an eagle – so near it was to being two aces in succession.

Jones was to pose no threat to the expatriate Scot, but his closest challenge still came from the amateur ranks, in the tall form and with the elegant swing of Oxford student Roger Wethered. Despite collecting a penalty shot for stepping on his ball in the third round Wethered's closing scores of 72 and 71 set Hutchison a stiff target. After a dreadful putting display in a third round 79, Hutchison needed a 70 to tie the young amateur, a score of three

Roger Wethered. In his youth, while still a student at Oxford, he lost the play-off for the 1921 Open to Jock Hutchison (INSET), who thus became the first non-British holder of the title – although he had in fact been born and raised in St Andrews and only later took American citizenship.

under par in those days. He knew exactly what was required and matched the target precisely. His fellow professionals rated it the greatest round of championship golf ever played.

Wethered was due to leave St Andrews as soon as the Championship was over so that he could play cricket for his local village team. He somewhat reluctantly stayed on for the 36-hole play-off, but was well beaten by a margin of nine shots by the experienced professional.

Bobby Jones had an unhappy first acquaintance with the Old Course. He arrived, at the age of nineteen, with a tremendous reputation as possibly the finest amateur golfer in America, although he had yet to win a national title. After two rounds he was the leading amateur, but 46 shots for the opening nine holes of the third round and a six at the almost driveable tenth hole led to a hasty retreat – he picked up his ball at the next hole and withdrew from the event. It was the only time in an illustrious career that he failed to complete a championship and it remained a lasting source of regret for the rest of his life.

His first emotion about the Old Course was that he 'hated it enthusiastically'. Yet he learned a lot about the control of his own temperament during that Open and he was to come to regard St Andrews as the greatest golfing challenge of them all.

Jones was the defending champion by the time he brought his father with him for the next St Andrews Open in 1927. He had first laid hands on the silver claret jug at Royal Lytham the year before, when a 150-yard bunker shot at the seventeenth hole secured victory over Al Watrous. A plaque on the bank of the bunker marks the spot to this day. Now at St Andrews to defend the title, he was also accompanied by the man from whom he had learned about golf. Stewart Maiden was a Scottish professional at the East Lakes Country Club, Atlanta, where young Bobby grew up. The family home was right on the golf course and although the young Jones boy never had a lesson from Maiden, he followed him around the course as a five-year-old and consciously copied his swing. 'It was my luck', he said many years later, 'to copy a man with the finest and soundest style.'

Stewart Maiden was known within the Jones entourage as 'Kiltie the King-Maker' and he was absolutely confident that his man would retain the title at the Home of Golf, the only firm prediction he ever made about the outcome of a championship. After an opening round of 68 Kiltie was jubilant, Jones stunned. On the largest greens in the world he had been wildly off-target with his approach play, normally such a strong part of his game. Maiden had suggested that if he started missing his shots to the green he might have more luck with his putting – and he was right. Jones holed a series of monsters – one of 120 feet for an eagle three at the fifth, five more of over 100 feet and nothing missed from twelve feet and under – for a total of 28 putts.

'It seems you can't play the other shots and putt all at once', he reflected after a brilliantly played third round of 73 which contained 36 putts. He need not have worried, his four-round total of 285 set a new record for the Championship and left his nearest challengers six shots behind.

The climax of Bobby Jones' career was to come three years later when he won the Amateur and Open Championships of both Britain and America in one incredible season. Part of that year's drama was again played out at St Andrews, but he retired from competitive golf at the end of the season, aged only 28, and was not part of the large American contingent which descended on the old, grey city in 1933. One reason for the size of the transatlantic invasion was the fourth match in the Ryder Cup series, played at Southport at the end of June, shortly before the Open. The home side scraped a one-point victory, Abe Mitchell disposing of Olin Dutra by nine and eight; but there were good wins for Americans Gene Sarazen, Walter Hagen, Craig Wood and Horton Smith.

One member of the American team who did not fare so well was Densmore Shute, who lost both his foursomes and singles matches. By three-putting the final green he had cost America the match. He might not have felt quite so disconsolate if he had known how fortune was to smile on him a few days later.

ABOVE *Bobby Jones, who gained his second Open title at St Andrews in 1927, pictured with Ben Sayers whose memories of the event went back over forty years.*
LEFT *Jones receives a ticker-tape welcome in the streets of New York after achieving his 'grand slam' in 1930.*

RIGHT *Watching the score board at the 1933 Open. The relaxed scene makes a vivid contrast with the frenetic atmosphere of today's Championships.*

BELOW *Craig Wood and Desmond Shute after the 1933 Open in which Shute defeated Wood by five shots in a play-off.*

Shute's progress in the Championship was unremarkable, never matching the leaders, but staying within striking distance with three steady rounds of 73. The more mercurial Sarazen ruined good scores in the second and final rounds with costly visits to the two most dangerous bunkers on the Old Course. In round two he found Hill bunker, deep below the left edge of the short eleventh and took three shots to get clear of the sand. Strongly in contention for the title in the final round he put his ball into Hell bunker and, in attempting to reach the green, ran up an eight. In fact, he could have played out safely for a six and still won.

The flamboyant Walter Hagen had led after rounds of 68 and 72 but mysteriously disappeared from the scene with lacklustre closing scores of 79 and 82. A fine third round of 68 had brought Craig Wood into the leading group and his chances of victory increased as British hopes Abe Mitchell and Henry Cotton squandered their lead with final rounds of 79. Wood could manage no better than 75 and, almost unnoticed, Shute scored his fourth consecutive 73 and tied for the title with his fellow American.

The 36-hole play-off started ominously for Wood, who opened with two sixes to Shute's well played fours. And it did not get any better. Rounds of 78 and 76 allowed Shute to play a conservative game and still win by five shots. The man who had come out of the Ryder Cup without a victory had captured a much bigger prize. It will have been no consolation to Craig Wood, but he did hit one of the longest drives ever recorded on the Old Course. Downwind on the hard fairway of the long fifth hole he drove 440 yards into the left-hand bunker on the ridge just short of the green in the final round. It cost him a stroke and possibly the Championship, but it is a shot still talked about to this day.

ST. ANDREWS

GUIDE FREE FROM TOWN CLERK, ST. ANDREWS, FIFE

Train services and fares from BRITISH RAILWAYS stations, offices and agencies

St Andrews offered an alluring prospect for holidaymakers in the bleak atmosphere of post-war Britain.

RIGHT *Dick Burton, who gained his Open title at St Andrews in 1939, shortly before the outbreak of the Second World War, defeating the American Johnny Bulla* (BELOW).

The next man to win the Championship at St Andrews held the title for a record number of years, but was unable to cash in on his success. The year was 1939 and within a matter of weeks of the contest Britain was at war with Germany.

Blunt-speaking Lancastrian Dick Burton was just the player to tame a lengthened Old Course in the bad weather conditions that prevailed in July of that year. Tall and powerful, he was one of the longest hitters in the British game, and it took all his skill and power to defeat American Johnny Bulla, another strong man of golf. Both the par-five holes, the fifth and fourteenth, had been lengthened since the Open was last played in St Andrews, effectively bringing the original bunkering back into play from the tee. Then as now, improved equipment had given professionals the ability to carry the ball beyond many long-standing hazards. The changes made little difference to the line of attack at the fifth, but against the wind at the fourteenth the group of bunkers in the left of the fairway, known as the Beardies, could now only be cleared by the strongest players. The out-of-bounds wall to the right was also brought more into play, and the gap between the two looked decidedly narrow.

Young South African Bobby Locke was heading for a great score when he reached the fourteenth tee in his first round, but became a victim of the Beardies and left his first recovery shot in the sand. When he did regain the fairway he ignored the safe route to the left and attempted the long carry over Hell bunker. Once more in sand, he finally escaped with an eight – yet still finished tied for the lead with Burton on 70. In the second round he was determined to avoid the Beardies at all costs and hit his tee shot over the out-of-bounds wall on to the Eden course. This time the hole cost him a seven and effectively ended his challenge.

At the start of the final round the field was led by Scotsman Johnny Fallon, with Bulla and Burton sharing fourth place. There was no question of the leaders going out at the end of the field in those days and Bulla was close to finishing his round as Burton was just setting out. This gave the Englishman a clear idea of what he needed to do to win as Fallon blew out of contention with a 79, leaving the two big hitters to decide the title. When he reached the final hole Burton needed a par four to win by a shot. He took the brave line along the fence with a drive of 300 yards, pitched to 15 feet and holed the putt. Within weeks he was serving with the Royal Air Force and he subsequently refused to be bitter about the lack of opportunity to exploit his potentially lucrative position as Champion. He took the wider view – he had survived the war while many of those who watched him win the Championship had not.

It was fitting that the first post-war championship should be held at the Home of Golf, ironic that it should be won by a man who thought little of the title, disliked the course and felt that the prize money was an insult.

Sam Snead had the smoothest, sweetest swing in the game. But he also had a quick and sometimes acid tongue. After a delayed flight from America he was rattling along the railway line which used to enter St Andrews through the heart of the links area when he got his first sight of the Old Course through the carriage window. He immediately endeared himself to local golfers, proud of their heritage and the standing of their world-famous course, by voicing the opinion that it must have been destroyed by enemy bombing during the war.

He may not have liked what he saw, but he had the power game to take advantage of the Old Course. Both the tenth and twelfth holes – par fours of more than 300 yards – were within his range that week and he knocked it on in two at the long fourteenth in all four rounds of the championship, two tremendous blows to cover 560 yards.

ABOVE *Bobby Locke pictured during the 1939 Open; he dropped out of contention in the second round but his time would come after the war, when he became a four-time winner of the title.*

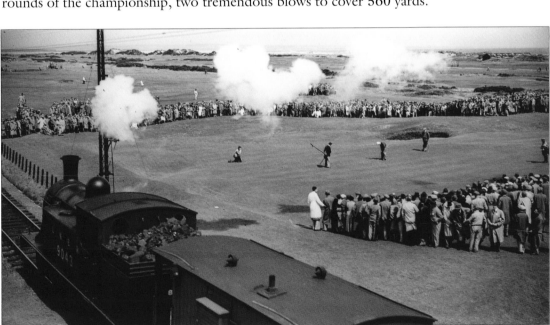

LEFT *This photograph, probably taken in the late 1940s or early 50s, conveys a vivid impression of the distractions players had to cope with when the railway line still ran into the city through the heart of the links.*

ABOVE RIGHT *Sam Snead, the 1946 Open Championship winner. The award ceremony* (ABOVE LEFT) *was delayed while Snead was tracked down to his hotel room.*

Despite his length he was not able to pull away from a good international entry and with one round to play he was tied with fellow American Johnny Bulla, who had finished second in the last pre-war Championship, and with the bustling little Welshman Dai Rees, who had equalled the course record 67 in the second round. Former champion Henry Cotton was one shot behind and South African Bobby Locke – a champion-in-waiting – was in close touch. Conditions on the final day were extremely tough on the outward holes and it was Locke who took the lead with a finely played level par 36.

Snead dropped four shots on those same nine holes and all the other leading players threw away their chances of a good score. Putting was one of the strongest parts of Locke's game, but on the easier downwind homeward stretch he completely lost his touch and allowed Snead a free run for the title. The American's 75 was good enough for a four-stroke winning margin.

When it was time for the presentation of the coveted trophy Snead was nowhere to be seen and the prize-giving had to be delayed while he was tracked down to his hotel. He was later to remark that at St Andrews he had won 'just another tournament' and that any time he left America he was 'camping out'. Not the most tactful comments about the Home of Golf at a time of severe food shortages so soon after the end of the war.

With additional courses being drafted on to the list of Championship venues, it was nine years before St Andrews next played host to the Open. By that time the reigning champion was the far more gracious young Australian Peter Thomson. A great supporter of links golf and the traditions of the game, he was not obsessed with power golf, often dropping down to a three-wood from the tee when he considered accuracy the better option. He was a pinpoint iron player and a wonderful judge of pace and line with running shots into links greens.

He was also something of an enigmatic character, with a wide range of interests outside golf – not one to spend hours in fruitless re-runs of great shots or missed opportunities. His style was uncomplicated and he played his shots with a notable lack of fuss or delay. He arrived in St Andrews as holder of the silver claret jug after a victory at Royal Birkdale the previous summer. American interest in the Championship was at a low ebb during this period and he faced a largely home-based challenge, boosted by entries from Argentinian Antonio Cerda, Flory van Donck of Belgium and, almost inevitably, Arthur D'Arcy Locke.

Locke had first appeared at St Andrews as a slim 22-year-old in the 1939 Open, when he finished a very creditable ninth behind Dick Burton. Immediately after the war he was second to Sam Snead and from 1949 had set an incredible record – winning the title three times in four years and never finishing lower than eighth place. It was assumed that he would provide the major opposition to Thomson's defence of the Championship, but in the event it was Scotland's Eric Brown who set the early pace with a fine opening 69. Locke saddled himself with a 74 from which he was never quite able to recover.

Another Scot, John Fallon, who had finished third in the pre-war Championship, had a second round 67 for a total of 140 – four under par. With Brown sharing the lead with Thomson at the halfway point, just one shot ahead of Fallon, it seemed that Scotland might achieve the home victory which had been denied them at St Andrews since James Braid's fifth and final title in 1910.

ABOVE Peter Thomson who took the 1955 Championship.
BELOW LEFT Thomson with Eric Brown, who shared the lead at the half-way point, and (RIGHT) playing his approach shot at the first hole.

But Thomson continued his steady progress, marred in the final round by bunker problems at the two long holes, but still setting a St Andrews record with a total of 281, four rounds of par and better. It was left to the 42-year-old Fallon to push him to the closing holes, his final 70 failing by one shot to catch the Australian, while Brown's challenge ended sadly with a 76. Locke finished fourth.

Thomson was to go on the following year to win his third successive title, placing his name in the record books alongside those of Young Tom Morris, Jamie Anderson and Bob Ferguson, and becoming the first player since 1882 to achieve such dominance. Having won at the Home of Golf and expressed his undoubted liking for the course, Thomson must have been delighted when a late decision was made to bring the Open back to St Andrews after a gap of only one year.

The venue for the 1957 Championship was largely decided by the unlikely figure of Egypt's President Nasser. By seizing control of the Suez Canal, in which the British Government had a major interest, he succeeded in precipitating panicky military reaction, the cutting off of oil supplies and, eventually, petrol rationing. Muirfield was to have been the scene of that year's Open, but the remote location of the course ruled it out of bounds with petrol restrictions in force. St Andrews, still well served by a railway which ran through the courses into the heart of the town, was the most logical alternative.

Virtually the same cast of players as two years before gathered in the old, grey city, with the addition of Americans Cary Middlecoff and Frank Stranahan. Yet it was to be the well known duo of Thomson and Locke who took centre stage once again. Between them they had won the Championship six times in the previous eight years, with three victories each. Locke was about to add a fourth. Thomson would go on to win two more.

Eric Brown played the supporting role for Scotland, leading after 36 holes with rounds of 67, 72. But Locke was six under par for the closing two rounds and swept through the field to win by three shots from Thomson. By this time Locke was a somewhat portly 40-year-old. His unhurried progress around the course, in voluminous plus-fours and white

The American challengers at the 1957 Open, Frank Stranahan (LEFT) *and Cary Middlecoff* (RIGHT).

The 40-year-old Bobby Locke on his way to becoming the 1957 Open Champion. Runner-up was Peter Thomson.

cap, could best be described as majestic. He hit all long shots with pronounced draw, starting his tee shots at the sixteenth hole of the Old Course well out over the railway line on the right and bringing the ball unerringly back into play.

Yet perhaps Locke was not as calm and composed as he always appeared, for the greatest drama was to come after the four rounds had been completed. He had finessed his second shot to the final hole within a few feet of the pin. He was asked to mark his ball two putter-head lengths away from another competitor's line. In the excitement of the moment he failed to replace his ball on its original spot before he putted out, a mistake only noticed some time later on news film of the event. The possibility of disqualification loomed over him, but the R & A committee quickly decided that he had gained no benefit from his innocent mistake and that, within the spirit of the game, the result should stand.

Had disqualification been imposed, Thomson would presumably have been awarded the title and the record books would now show that he won five Championships in succession, for he was the victor the following year at Royal Lytham. The Australian said later: 'I don't know what I would have done if they had disqualified Bobby. I certainly would not have wanted to win the Championship that way.'

With an act of compassion and an expression of true sportsmanship a dramatic era of championship golf at St Andrews came to a close. It was to give way to a period of explosive growth in the game – led by the strong personality and aggressive golf of Arnold Palmer.

Chapter 6

OPEN CHAMPIONSHIPS III

T HE 'SWINGING SIXTIES' was a phrase coined to celebrate the musical, sexual and fashion freedoms of a decade which seemed determined to shake off the clinging aftermath of world war and head full speed into the future. But it was an expression that could also have been applied specifically to golf; for this was the period when the popularity of the game blossomed as never before, triggering an explosion of interest which is still gathering momentum today. Like the ripples from a giant rock cast into a still pool, the effect continues to sweep over ever-more-distant shores, bringing the ancient game of golf to a continually expanding audience.

This new-found impetus came at an appropriate time. For in July of 1960, one hundred years after the first Open Championship was played at Prestwick, the centenary event was held over the Old Course. It was to be an intriguing battle between the old and the new forces in golf.

The old guard were represented by four-time champions Peter Thomson and Bobby Locke, well supported by players who had won many tournaments and often been in contention for the Open Championship, but who had never quite cleared the final hurdle – characters like Roberto de Vicenzo of Argentina, Scotland's Eric Brown, Welshmen Dai Rees and Dave Thomas, Benard Hunt and Peter Alliss of England and Ireland's Christy O'Connor.

The young Turks were led by an intense young South African, Gary Player, who had won the title a year earlier at Muirfield after being told just a few seasons before by an eminent British professional that he would never be a successful golfer and should go home and take up another career.

But most significant of all was the entry of a 30-year-old American, Arnold Palmer. He had been US Amateur Champion in 1954 and had won a handful of tournaments on the American circuit since turning professional, including his first major success – the capture of the US Masters title in 1958. Then in the spring of 1960 he won the Masters again and followed up two months later with a spectacular victory in the US Open Championship where, seven shots behind leader Mike Souchak going into the final round, Palmer unleashed one

The Centenary Open at St Andrews, 1960, in which Arnold Palmer represented a new generation of golfers. INSET *Gene Sarazen, the veteran who played successfully in the pre-qualifying rounds, but then decided that his 'old legs' were not up to a further four rounds on the Old Course, and withdrew.*

ABOVE *St Andrews,
1960. Arnold Palmer
(left) with Frank
Stranahan (centre) and
Gary Player.*
INSETS *Two of the other
challengers for the 1960
Open: Argentinian
Roberto de Vicenzo (left)
and Australian Kel
Nagle (right).*

of the charges that were to bring him lasting fame and cut through the field with a 65. Suddenly Palmer was the hottest property in golf and his appearance at St Andrews did much to revivify interest in the British Open. Since Sam Snead's victory in 1946 and Ben Hogan's lone success in 1953 the leading American professionals had chosen to by-pass the world's oldest championship. As the US was, during that period, the strongest golfing nation, their absence took away much of the status and prestige of the Open. The event had become something of a domestic and Commonwealth affair, rather than a truly international championship; saved from parochialism, to some extent, only by the domination of two truly world-class golfers in Thomson and Locke.

Palmer not only represented the might of American golf, he was the charismatic new leader of the pack. His style of play was raw, a flat, quick, truncated swing that made the purists of the British establishment wince. His advice to youngsters was to hit the ball hard and then learn to control it. And that was the way he played – crashing the ball into seemingly unplayable positions and then conjuring it on to the green with a mixture of brute force, imagination and extreme delicacy. Televised golf was relatively new on both sides of the Atlantic, but Palmer sent the ratings soaring as people who had never played golf switched on in their millions to watch the new sporting hero.

With expectations high in anticipation of a classic battle between the powerful new players and the experienced masters of links golf, it was typical that, when he emerged, the new champion should turn out to be a virtual unknown.

Kel Nagle had partnered his more illustrious fellow Australian Peter Thomson to two World Cup victories by the time he arrived in St Andrews for the Centenary Open, but his earlier forays in British tournaments had been unfruitful and his chances of success were not even considered, except by the shrewd Thomson, who had a worthwhile wager on his compatriot at very long odds.

The final two rounds of the Championship were still played in one day in 1960 – at least that was the way it was planned. But as the morning round finished the Old Course vanished under water. Torrential rain swept down the road behind the R & A clubhouse, cascaded down the steps and flooded the Valley of Sin, the depression that fronts the final green, to a depth of three feet.

As the fire brigade pumped away the floods and green-keepers mopped and swept in an attempt to get the course ready for the fourth round on the following day, the completed third-round scores showed that Nagle had taken a two-shot lead over early front runner Roberto de Vicenzo and headed Palmer by four. Those who expected the Australian to crumble under the weight of a Palmer onslaught did not understand that this was a man who actually thrived on competitive pressure, unlike the majority of tournament players, who wage a constant and increasingly futile battle against nervous tension. Having been a long hitter and poor putter in his younger days, Nagle was now moderate but accurate with his long game and deadly on the greens. Palmer lived up to his reputation, finishing with a birdie for a fighting 68. The cheer that erupted around the eighteenth as he holed his final putt carried a clear message to Nagle.

At that moment he was studying the line of a 10-foot putt at the seventeenth. He had to hole that putt and par the last hole to win. He did both with calm assurance to make the giant leap from being a modestly successful tournament player to conqueror of the oldest championship. In the following six years he was twice fifth, took fourth place on two other occasions and was once runner-up. Four years later he won the Canadian Open and the following year came close to adding the US Open title, losing in a play-off with Gary Player. He may have been unknown when he arrived in St Andrews, but his baptism of fire on the Old Course led to a glittering career.

Arnold Palmer had come within a shot of victory at St Andrews and had brought a new spark of life to the oldest championship – the lead he gave to American participants has been followed ever since by that country's greatest players. Foiled once, he was not to be denied again, and won the title in the following two years at Royal Birkdale and Troon. When he returned to the Home of Golf for his farewell appearance in the 1990 Championship his reception was as warm and enthusiastic as it had been thirty years earlier.

ABOVE *Kel Nagle, the victor at St Andrews in 1960.*

BELOW *Arnold Palmer's farewell appearance at St Andrews for the 1990 Open. The Palmer magic continued to grip a younger generation of fans.*

Strangely, because of ill-health and tiredness, Palmer was not in the American contingent which contested the 1964 Open at St Andrews, but the new giant of American golf, Jack Nicklaus, was. So, too, was a tall, slim Californian with a wonderfully rhythmic swing. He had finished second to Nicklaus in the previous year's Masters and fifth in the US Open. His name was Tony Lema and his performance at St Andrews was to stun the golfing world.

Arriving in time for only two practice rounds, Lema said: 'I came chiefly to visit. St Andrews is the Home of Golf and I felt I should see it for myself.' In fact he had the benefit of two priceless assets – his own tremendous ability and the best caddie in the business. Four-handicap local golfer Tip Anderson had been Palmer's regular partner since the Centenary Open. In Palmer's absence, Anderson was able to choose between carrying the bag for Nicklaus or Lema and, unsure that the immensely powerful game of Nicklaus was suited to the subtleties of the Old Course, he chose to go with a man he had never seen in action. Anderson was immediately impressed with the accuracy of Lema's driving and the fantastic control he had with the wedge. Within hours of stepping on to a links course for the first time he was able to play the all-important pitch and run shot with absolute confidence.

The 1964 Open at St Andrews attracted a strong American challenge, including Jack Nicklaus (RIGHT) *and Tony Lema* (BELOW), *who was to carry off the trophy.*

In return, Lema was delighted with Anderson's intimate knowledge of the course and his uncanny ability to hand him the right club. As he shared two cases of champagne with the press – a winning habit which earned him the nickname 'Champagne Tony' – he commented: 'Tip Anderson was far more useful to me than anyone can possibly imagine. Without his help I doubt if I could have won.'

Lema also had a little bit of luck, drawing an early starting time in the first round on a day when the strong wind made the course very tough. Those who went out later took the brunt of the gale, which developed around lunchtime. So Lema was back in the clubhouse with a workman-like 73 while Nicklaus was battling sixty-mile-an-hour winds which whipped sand out of the bunkers, tossed pitch shots backwards, rolled balls off greens and demolished tents. Nevertheless, Nicklaus's score of 76 was a miracle of control; he flighted the ball low through the wind in defiance of the pundits who had forecast that he would be unable to adapt his normal high shot trajectory, and his score would have been better if the severe conditions had not destroyed his normally precise putting touch.

Although conditions eased on the second day, Nicklaus again caught the worst of the weather and his putting was even more disastrous. He three-putted seven times in the opening two rounds and had only three single putts, the longest from 5 feet. His rounds of 76 and 74 put him nine shots behind Lema, whose second round 68 gave him a two-stroke lead over the field. At the fourteenth hole the helping wind had dropped considerably, but Lema still covered the 560 yards with an enormous drive and a six-iron.

The golf played by the two Americans on the final day was spell-binding. Nicklaus was ten under par for the 36 holes, with fantastic rounds of 66 and 68, but made up only four shots on his rival. Lema had a rather shaky start, dropping two shots in the opening four holes, but quickly recovered with a run of five threes from the seventh. His 68 gave away only two shots of his massive lead over Nicklaus and in the final round a calmly played 70 gave him victory by five strokes.

Nicklaus had arrived at St Andrews with a reputation for prodigious power; even so, when he drove the final green in the first two rounds many thought it could only have been achieved with the strong wind at his back. But on the final day, in much calmer conditions, he did it twice more. The hole measured 381 yards for that championship.

Tony Lema made a spirited defence of his crown the following year at Royal Birkdale, leading after two rounds, but being overtaken by Peter Thomson, who captured his fifth title. It was to be Lema's last appearance in the Open, for the talented, easy-going and likeable champion was killed in a plane crash the following year. Yet his personality and his golf were still vividly remembered when the Open returned to St Andrews in 1970.

Bernard Hunt, one of the leading British professionals in the 1960s. Hunt finished fourth behind Tony Lema of the USA in the 1964 Open.

Tony Jacklin, the reigning Champion, who met with initial triumph and ultimate disaster at the 1970 Open.

By then Britain had a home-grown champion. Tony Jacklin, with his fine victory at Royal Lytham the previous July, had become the first British winner since Max Faulkner in 1951. And he had gone on to win the US Open title by seven shots just a few weeks before arriving in St Andrews. At the start of his first round it looked as if he might retain his title in impressive style. He birdied the first three holes and had added two more by the time he reached the ninth, where a slightly pulled one-iron from the tee left him in the light heather exactly 103 yards from the pin. His wedge shot pitched just short, hit the stick and dropped into the hole. He had played the first nine holes of the Old Course in 29 shots, seven under par.

He picked up another birdie at the tenth, but the sky was getting darker by the minute and thunder was crackling on the horizon. After three solid pars and a good drive at the fourteenth he was at the top of his backswing with a three-wood when someone shouted 'Fore!' He made solid contact, but the ball flew well right, landing in a gorse bush on mounds just short of the green.

By the time he reached his ball the rain was lashing down and within minutes parts of the green were under water. Play was finally abandoned for the day and scheduled to resume at 7.30 the next morning. But by then the magic had evaporated. He took a penalty drop from the bush, pitched on and missed the putt, three-putted the sixteenth and dropped another shot at the Road Hole. At eight under par after thirteen holes anything had seemed possible. In the cold, wet and windy conditions the next morning a round of 67 was a massive disappointment, and although he battled away through the four rounds for fifth place, just three shots behind the leaders, he must often reflect on what might have happened if rain had not stopped play on that first day.

While Jacklin's drama came at the beginning of the Championship, the fates kept Doug Sanders waiting until the closing minutes before administering the sickening blow which is still remembered by everyone who plays the game as 'that putt'.

It was the end of the fourth round. Lee Trevino had blown his lead with a 77. Jacklin was a shot further back. As Jack Nicklaus played the final hole he was just one stroke behind Doug Sanders; he drove into the Valley of Sin at the front of the green and three-putted. Sanders needed a par four to win.

He hit a fine drive and elected to pitch over the Valley of Sin with a sand wedge, but failed to get any bite in the shot and finished 30 feet behind the hole. The slope down to the hole is less severe than it appears and he left his approach putt just over 3 feet short. He admitted later that he mis-hit the second putt, which slipped away to the right of the hole. His wife had been unable to watch, but knew instantly, from the sympathetic groan from the crowd, that he would have to face Nicklaus in a play-off.

Four shots behind after thirteen holes the next day, Sanders' chances of Open glory looked slim, but he hung in doggedly and reduced the deficit to just one shot as they reached the eighteenth. Sanders hit his tee shot slightly closer to the green than he had on the previous afternoon. Nicklaus peeled off his bright-yellow sweater and smashed a tremendous shot right through the green and into the rough on the banking at the back – a few more feet and he would have been out of bounds.

Sanders then played a near-perfect chip and run shot to 3 feet and must have cursed his decision the day before when he chose to fly the ball into the green rather than playing the easier and safer running shot.

Nicklaus realized that he had to get down in two or face an extended play-off. He certainly could not count on Sanders missing another short putt on this green. His recovery shot with a wedge stopped 7 feet short of the hole and he was now faced with a longer version of the downhill, left-to-right putt that had killed Sanders' chances in the fourth round. It nearly got away from him, catching the right edge of the hole before dropping from sight.

Nicklaus, normally in ice-cool control of his emotions, tossed his putter high in the air. Both he and the unfortunate Sanders had to take evasive action as it came thudding down. 'I didn't realize I had thrown my putter,' he confessed. 'I've never done anything like that before.'

Winning the oldest championship at the Home of Golf can have strange effects on even the most controlled individuals. Losing the title by missing a short putt on the final green can blight a career. Walter Hagen used to say that nobody remembered who came second. Sanders is proof of the fallacy of that remark.

Doug Sanders driving off during the 1970 Open and (INSET) *demonstrating the length of the infamous putt which cost him the title.*

Nicklaus had been suffering, by his own incredible standards, something of a crisis before his 1970 victory. It had been three years since he had last added a major championship to the already impressive total – eight in all – gained during his years of domination between 1962–7. He was in exactly the same situation when the Open came back to St Andrews in 1978. His tally of major victories had by now increased to fourteen, but he had not added to it for three years. He had come very close twelve months earlier when he and Tom Watson had left the rest of the field in their wake as they fought out a tremendous duel at Turnberry; only a missed short putt by Nicklaus at the seventeenth separated them at the climax.

Now Watson was defending that hard-won title at St Andrews against a high quality international field. After three rounds it seemed that the dramatic events at Turnberry might be repeated. Watson was in the lead at five under par and Nicklaus just one shot behind. But this time they were not alone – only two shots separated the leading 10 players. Watson shared the lead with British giant Peter Oosterhuis, a talented player who had an unfortunate tendency to block tee shots out to the right at moments of great pressure – and that is the side where most danger lurks at St Andrews. Nicklaus was joined in second spot by New Zealander Simon Owen, experienced American Ben Crenshaw and leading Japanese money-winner Isao Aoki. Nick Faldo, Tom Kite and former champion Tom Weiskopf were hovering ominously just two strokes off the lead.

Yet the expected battle between the two leading Americans failed to ignite. Watson seemed curiously unable to cope with a change of wind direction and slipped rapidly out of contention to finish with a 76 and a share of fourteenth place. Ray Floyd did the reverse, coming out of the pack with a fine 68 to set an early target of 283, a total only Nicklaus would get below. Owen, who had added two European tour victories to his home successes in New Zealand, was paired with Nicklaus, and moved into a one-stroke lead after five successive threes from

Two famous victories separated by an eight-year gap – Jack Nicklaus poses after his 1970 triumph and (INSET) holds the claret cup aloft after winning again in 1978.

St Andrews 1978. The strong field included Tom Watson (LEFT), Tom Kite (RIGHT), and Peter Oosterhuis (INSET CENTRE) as well as the young Seve Ballesteros (BELOW).

the eighth and a chip-in birdie at the fifteenth. Then the wheels came off. His sand wedge approach to the next hole scampered through the back of the green and he took three to get down while Nicklaus holed a 6-foot birdie putt to regain the lead.

Owen also fell foul of the seventeenth, overhitting his second shot on to the road behind the green and dropping two shots behind Nicklaus, who claimed his second St Andrews title with a cast-iron four at the final hole. Owen's moment of glory was gone and he shared second place with Floyd, Crenshaw and Kite.

Seve Ballesteros, then only 21 but heading towards his third successive title as European number one, might have been in closer contention had he not continually fallen foul of the seventeenth hole. This 461-yard par four demands a perfectly placed tee shot in the right side of the fairway over what used to be the old railway yards – now the grounds of the Old Course Hotel. The second shot must then find a narrow shelf of green, angled away behind a deep bunker and backed by a pathway, road and out-of-bounds wall.

'It is a par five to me,' said the young Spaniard, and proved it throughout the week, as well as racking up an out-of-bounds six in the second round. He was in good company. 'It may be a famous hole, but I don't like it,' was Arnold Palmer's comment after twice hitting his drives into the hotel gardens. One of the leading Japanese players, Tommy Nakajima, took several incautious blows to extricate himself from the Road Hole bunker and blew away his chances with a nine, while heavyweight Scotsman Brian Barnes had the distinction of hitting the green in two and putting into the same bunker for an eventual six.

The seventeenth is a hole always guaranteed to cause heartache and controversy, and it was to cost Tom Watson the next St Andrews Open in the summer of 1984. He dropped three shots there in the opening two rounds, but thought he had laid the ghost with a solid par four in the third. At the end of that round he was tied for the lead with virtually unknown Australian Ian Baker-Finch, known on tour as 'Hyphen'. He had taken advantage of practice rounds with former champions and fellow Australians Peter Thomson and Kel Nagle to play the course patiently and with respect. His fine iron play and excellent putting had given him a three-round total of eleven under par.

Two shots behind were Seve Ballesteros and Bernhard Langer, with the rest of the field a further five shots down and effectively out of the hunt. It was heady company for the inexperienced Australian and he walked straight into problems at the start. His approach to the first spun back viciously into the burn and he was never able to regain his confidence, eventually finishing in joint eighth place.

In the match in front Langer hit a string of superb iron shots into the greens on the outward nine holes, but failed to hole any of the short birdie putts and consequently was never quite close enough to mount a challenge.

Watson had a definite edge over Ballesteros as he stood on the twelfth tee, but in going for a big drive at a par-four hole which is just about within reach for the longer professionals he finished in an unplayable lie in the whins. The penalty drop cost him a five and the two men were level when they reached the seventeenth.

The 1984 Open brought a host of stars to St Andrews including Bernhard Langer (ABOVE) *and Seve Ballesteros, who is seen* (BELOW RIGHT) *holing a birdie putt at the eighteenth to take the title.*

It was not a favourite hole for either player. Ballesteros kept his tee shot well left and found a good lie in the rough. This is essentially the wrong side of the fairway, but he hit a flier with his six-iron which reached the top level of the green almost 200 yards away. Two putts gave him his first four at the hole.

Watson took the more direct line from the tee, flirting with the out of bounds on the right and finishing in the perfect position in the fairway from which to attack the green. He was no further from the green than Ballesteros had been moments earlier, but he chose to flight the ball into the breeze with a two-iron. His ball cleared the green, bounced on the road and settled in grass just two feet from the wall at the back. He could do no more than stab the ball on to the green and two-putt for a five. A great roar from the final green left him in no doubt that Seve had finished with a birdie. His only hope was to hole his second shot. From 93 yards he was exactly on line, but strong. His attempt to win a sixth Open title had been frustrated by the devilish seventeenth.

St Andrews, 1984. The seventeenth hole (LEFT) *was to cost Tom Watson the title; here it is being played by Hale Irwin, who found himself on the wrong side of the road in the course of one of his rounds.* BELOW LEFT *Seve with Spanish friends including Manuel Pinero in yellow.*

ABOVE *Ian Baker-Finch ('Hyphen' to his friends) who faded out of contention after an impressive opening round.*

87

There were no such problems for the man who won the 24th Open Championship to be played over the Old Course – Nick Faldo, title holder in 1990. Not since Tony Lema's outstanding win in 1964 had the Old Course been treated to such a display of precision driving and superlative iron play as Faldo demonstrated that year. But he had set a game plan for the entire course – and particularly for the dreaded Road Hole.

He determined to treat it as a par four-and-a-half – always choosing a club for his second shot which would not reach the bunker or the road. His intention was to play for the front right side of the green and take his chances of making four by chipping close. He did not exactly beat the hole into submission, but he did not make any stupid mistakes either. It was a measure of his domination that he was only once in sand, to the left of the fourth green in the final round, and on the largest putting surfaces in the world he did not three-putt once in 72 holes.

Scoring was exceptionally low, the half-way cut coming at one under par and Faldo's total of 270 – 18 under par – broke the previous record for the Championship over the Old Course by six shots. His first round of 67 finished with a flourish, his pitch and run shot to the final green rolling straight into the hole for an eagle two. Yet it was not good enough to take the lead. Big-hitting Australian Greg Norman opened with a 66 and repeated it on the second day. Faldo immediately went one better with a 65.

The two were paired together the next day, when Faldo virtually won the Championship in a stunning third round. By the ninth he was three shots ahead and as Norman stumbled and staggered to an inward half of 40, Faldo kept up the pressure. It was no contest – Faldo 67; Norman 76.

ABOVE *1990 was Nick Faldo's year; he was paired with Greg Norman* (BELOW RIGHT) *in the third round and shot 67 to Norman's 76.*

In the meantime Ian Baker-Finch, who had figured so prominently in the previous Open at St Andrews, had snatched seven birdies and an eagle in his opening 12 holes and completed the course in 64 for a total of 204. But despite these and many other heroics, Faldo started the final day on an unprecedented score of 199, with a five-shot advantage over the field.

At one point on that final day colourful American Payne Stewart, in a startling Stars and Stripes plus-fours outfit, came within two shots of the Englishman, but a confident six-iron to eight feet for a birdie at the fifteenth hole steadied Faldo, and his five-shot margin at the end of the Championship was just reward for a week of exceptional golf.

The Old Course at St Andrews has produced some of the finest moments in the long and challenging history of the world's oldest championship. It will continue to do so for as long as the game is played.

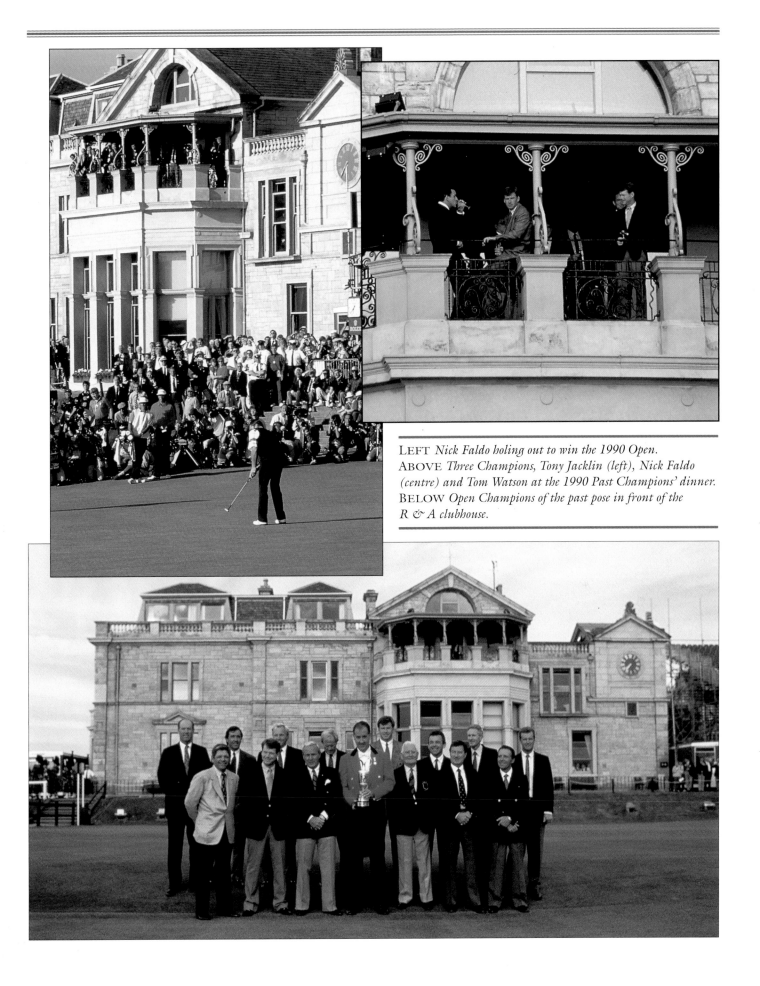

LEFT *Nick Faldo holing out to win the 1990 Open.*
ABOVE *Three Champions, Tony Jacklin (left), Nick Faldo (centre) and Tom Watson at the 1990 Past Champions' dinner.*
BELOW *Open Champions of the past pose in front of the R & A clubhouse.*

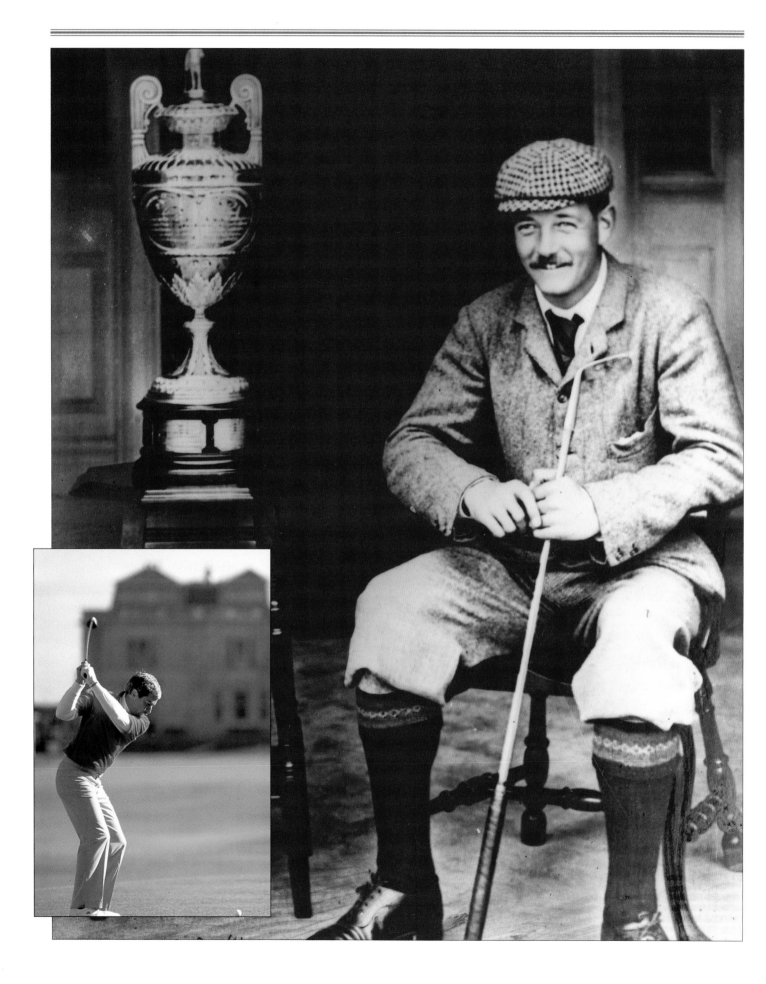

Chapter 7

MAJOR CHAMPIONSHIPS

A S THE INTERNATIONALLY ACCEPTED Home of Golf, St Andrews has, not unnaturally, been the venue for a vast range of events in addition to the regular playing of the Open Championship over the ancient course. Yet surprisingly few have been professional tournaments, and it seems strange that such prestigious confrontations as the Ryder Cup and the World Cup have never been staged on the Old Course.

The first event 'open to all gentlemen players' on the Old Course was a 'Grand National Tournament' in 1857, and this event – nothing to do with horse racing – was repeated in the two subsequent years. These contests were clear forerunners of the Amateur Championship and pre-dated the first Open at Prestwick by three years. Yet the idea behind the event came from the Prestwick club which suggested that it be held 'either at St Andrews or Prestwick as may be determined by a majority of the competing clubs.'

These amateur events were a far cry from the created-for-television Alfred Dunhill Cup which has made the Old Course its permanent home since its inauguration in 1985. The event brings together three-man teams from 16 nations in an odd medal match-play format which guarantees that each game goes the full 18 holes by pitting a player's medal score against that of his opponent. Australia, England, Ireland and the United States have shared the honours equally, with the Swedes confirming their emergence as a golfing nation by securing victory in 1991, and Canada beating America in 1994. The host nation has twice reached the final, losing on both occasions to the old enemy from south of the border – by two matches to one in 1987 and by two matches to nil, with one halved, in 1992.

It was during the 1987 Dunhill cup that Curtis Strange set a new record for the Old Course. On a slightly damp and misty October day, when not a breath of wind disturbed the air, he added spice to the anticlimactic play-off for third and fourth place, beating Greg Norman by eight shots with an incredible round of 62.

Freddie Tait, who set the Old Course record in 1890 with 77, which he lowered in 1894 to 72. INSET *Curtis Strange, who reduced the Old Course record to 62 in 1987.*

ALFRED DUNHILL CUP

	THURSDAY	FRIDAY	SATURDAY	SUNDAY		SATURDAY	FRIDAY	THURSDAY

GROUP 1 / GROUP 1 / GROUP 1 — SEMI-FINAL — GROUP 3 / GROUP 3 / GROUP 3

ZIMBABWE 0 · ZIMBABWE 2 · ARGENTINA 0
IRELAND 3 · ARGENTINA 1 · IRELAND 3
SPAIN 2 · SPAIN 1 · ZIMBABWE 2
ARGENTINA 1 · IRELAND 3 · SPAIN 1

SEMI-FINAL: IRELAND — ENGLAND

FINAL

WALES 1 · UNITED STATES 2 · SCOTLAND 1
PARAGUAY 2 · PARAGUAY 1 · PARAGUAY 2
UNITED STATES 3 · SCOTLAND 3 · UNITED STATES 3
SCOTLAND 0 · WALES 0 · WALES 0

GROUP 2 / GROUP 2 / GROUP 2 — SEMI-FINAL — GROUP 4 / GROUP 4 / GROUP 4

SOUTH AFRICA 2 · SOUTH AFRICA 1 · ENGLAND 1
CHINESE TAIPEI 0 · MEXICO 2 · SOUTH AFRICA 2
ENGLAND 3 · ENGLAND 3 · MEXICO 2
MEXICO 0 · CHINESE TAIPEI 0 · CHINESE TAIPEI 0

SEMI-FINAL: UNITED STATES — SWEDEN

CANADA 2 · AUSTRALIA 3 · AUSTRALIA 1
JAPAN 1 · JAPAN 2 · CANADA 2
AUSTRALIA 1 · SWEDEN 2 · SWEDEN 3
SWEDEN 2 · CANADA 1 · JAPAN 0

The Dunhill Cup has become an annual event on the Old Course since its inauguration in 1985.

TOP *The three-man teams come to St Andrews from all corners of the globe.*

CENTRE *Christy O'Connor Jr, representing Ireland in the 1989 event.*

BELOW LEFT *The Irish team, winners in 1990 (from left to right): Ronan Rafferty, David Feherty and Pip Walton.*

BELOW RIGHT *(left to right) Curtis Strange, Mark Calcavechia and Tom Kite, the American victors in 1989.*

Even with a prize fund of £1 million, Dunhill have not found it possible to attract all the world's leading players to the Home of Golf towards the end of a long season. That was also a problem for the inaugural Alcan Golfer of the Year event in 1967, when Arnold Palmer, Jack Nicklaus and Gary Player all spurned the chance to win the seemingly massive £20,000 first prize.

There was an ironic outcome to the Alcan tournament. In reality it was two events in one – the Golfer of the Year title being contested by a supposedly elite field and the Alcan International decided among the lesser fry. They all played over the Old Course on the same days. Australian Peter Thomson, who had won the fifth of his Open Championship titles only two years before at Royal Birkdale, was not included in the main event. He was relegated to the supporting feature where the first prize was £2,500.

Gay Brewer, then the reigning Masters Champion, won the Golfer of the Year award after tying with Billy Casper on 283. But there was consternation and embarrassment on the faces of the sponsors when Thomson finished two shots better on 281, collecting the secondary prize together with the bonus for the week's lowest aggregate score. 'Just call me Golfer of the Week', he said, tongue in cheek, at the prize-giving. It was a remark which did not go down well in all quarters. American pro Mason Rudolf, who finished on 294, thirteen shots behind Thomson, muttered: 'It's nice to see him win. I've been playing the US circuit for nine years and I've never seen him win before.'

It is worth recording a curious footnote to the short-lived Alcan event, which was to survive only three more years. Kel Nagle, who had won the Centenary Open at St Andrews in 1960 and gone on to become one of the game's most successful players throughout that decade, was credited with a score of 105, an apparent catastrophe that was due to a slip of Christy O'Connor's pencil rather than a complete collapse of the Australian's game. O'Connor was Nagle's playing partner and inadvertently put his first-nine score in the space opposite the ninth hole. Nagle signed the card without realizing the error and, under the rules of golf, the massive total had to stand.

Despite Mason Rudolf's dismissive remark, Peter Thomson's record in world golf was mightily impressive, and he was something of a St Andrews specialist. Before his Alcan victory he had won the Martini International over the Old Course in 1962, finished second in the 1957 Open to Bobby Locke and had won the Championship there two years before.

Thomson's earliest triumph dates back to 1954, the only time the Match-play Championship was played at St Andrews, when he won the final at the second extra hole against Scotsman John Fallon. In an earlier round Thomson had been two down with two to play against Scots hero John Panton, but he finished with two birdie threes to square the match and finally holed a monster putt at the fourth for victory.

There was an even better finish in store for another Australian when the Scottish Open was played on the Old Course in 1973. Graham Marsh hit a drive and an eight-iron to the notorious seventeenth and holed out from twelve feet, then drove the final green and rolled in a 30-footer – a birdie, eagle finish that deservedly earned him the title.

Charlie Ward, winner of the Daily Mail Victory Tournament in 1945.
INSET *Vicente Fernandez of Argentina, who held off a strong challenge from Gary Player to win the PGA Championship on the Old Course in 1979.*

A pitch-and-putt four at that dreaded seventeenth hole allowed Vicente Fernandez of Argentina to stay one stroke ahead of a charging Gary Player for the PGA Championship of 1979. Although played in May the event ran into a week of biting cold and unrelenting wind, conditions that should have favoured the power players. But Fernandez, at 5 feet 7 inches and less than 150 pounds, controlled the ball magnificently for his win.

An equally diminutive figure, English professional Charlie Ward, won the only other professional events held at St Andrews. He was still serving in the Royal Air Force when the Daily Mail Victory tournament was played in 1945. Due to a modest celebration of his triumph in this first post-war event he was late in reporting back to his unit. The story of his victory cut no ice with his commanding officer and he was confined to barracks as a punishment. It was probably the memory of that punishment that brought him back to the Old Course four years later and inspired him to win the Dunlop Masters over the world's most famous course.

Despite all the heroics of the modern professional game, the outcome of the 1930 Amateur Championship probably has as much significance in the history of St Andrews as any event played over the Old Course.

That was the year when Bobby Jones achieved the impossible – winning the Amateur and Open Championships of both Britain and America in one incredible season. Some commentators called it the 'impregnable quadrilateral'. Others, with an eye for a more graphic phrase, tagged it 'the grand slam'. The latter expression was in fact invented by Jones' close friend, the golf writer O.B. Keeler, to describe what he believed to be an impossible achievement. When Jones proved him wrong he felt that the term was 'too casual for the supreme feat of the sporting world'.

When Jones arrived in St Andrews that summer he had just won the US Amateur for the fifth time. He had already captured the US Open three times and the British Open twice. But he had never been successful in the British Amateur.

In his first-round match he drove into Cottage bunker from the fourth tee, a distance of close to 300 yards, and covered the next 120 yards with a pitch into the hole. The toughest of the eight matches he had to play to win the Championship came in the fourth round, when he was matched against defending champion Cyril Tolley. All square as they played the seventeenth, Jones had a stroke of luck when his shot to the green hit a spectator and stopped short of the road which runs close behind the putting surface. Tolley was just short of the Road Hole bunker and played what he later described as the finest shot he ever made, pitching over the sand to the narrowest part of the green and leaving the ball no more than 2 feet from the hole. Jones put himself under tremendous pressure when he left his simple approach shot 8 feet short, but resolutely holed out and finally took the match with a stymie on the first extra hole, leaving his first putt between Tolley's ball and the hole. In those days there was no provision for marking and lifting the ball; Tolley needed to chip over Jones' ball into the hole and he failed.

The 36-hole final was something of an anticlimax, despite the fact that Jones' opponent was former champion Roger Wethered. Jones was three under par when he won by seven and six to clinch the one title which had eluded him in seven years of domination at the highest levels of the game.

1930 was Bobby Jones' annus mirabilis, his four titles included the British Amateur Championship at St Andrews. INSET Jones with his fellow finalist, the British amateur, Roger Wethered.

The Amateur Championship was inaugurated by the Royal Liverpool Golf Club at Hoylake in 1885, the second event coming to St Andrews in September the following year only after it was withdrawn from North Berwick at six weeks' notice because 'The dates originally suggested have been found to be inconvenient.' In all, the Championship has been played fifteen times over the Old Course.

The competition was open to all amateur golfers who were members of any golf club, and an amateur was defined as:

A golfer who has never made for sale golf clubs, balls or any other article connected with the game; who has never carried clubs for hire, or received any consideration for playing in a match, or for giving lessons in the game; and who, for a period of five years, has never received a money prize in any open competition.

95

Two great Amateur Champions from the Edwardian era, Harold Hilton (LEFT) winner in 1901, and John Ball (RIGHT) who had his sixth victory at St Andrews in 1907. INSET The British Amateur Championship trophy, featuring Old Tom Morris on the top.

Horatio Hutchinson, better known as Horace, lost the first Amateur by a margin of seven and six, but beat Henry Lamb by the same score to win at St Andrews in 1886, and successfully defended the title the following year back at Hoylake. He spent more time practising putting than any other aspect of the game and developed a very wristy action, which is contrary to all modern teaching. But he was reckoned to be the finest putter since Young Tom Morris.

The inventor of the overlapping grip which was made popular by Harry Vardon and which bears his name today, was, in fact, John Laidlay. He won the Amateur at St Andrews in 1889 and 1891 and was beaten in the finals three times.

Leslie Balfour-Melville, the Amateur Champion of 1895 with a last hole victory at St Andrews over John Ball, was not only a prolific winner of club events within the Royal and Ancient and the Honourable Company of Edinburgh Golfers, but a fine cricketer who scored a century against the MCC at Lords.

By the time Harold Hilton won the Amateur over the Old Course in 1901 he had already become one of only three amateurs to win the Open Championship, a feat he had achieved twice. He was to win the amateur crown four times in all, the last at St Andrews in 1913 when he was 44 years old. He went on to become editor of two golf magazines.

The only other amateurs to win the Open were Bobby Jones and John Ball, who matched Jones in one respect by winning both the Amateur and Open titles in one season. Ball set many other records, his victory at St Andrews in 1907 being the sixth of his eight triumphs in the event. He was 51 when he beat Abe Mitchell for his last title.

Between the two world wars, Bobby Jones' extraordinary feats in 1930 dominated the amateur scene in St Andrews, but there were also victories by Ernest Holderness (later to be knighted) in 1924 and by Scotsman Hector Thomson in 1936. Both played in Walker Cup matches for Britain against America, but Sir Ernest retired early from competitive golf while Thomson went on to become a successful professional.

In 1948 the Amateur at St Andrews was captured by an American who was more professional than most pros. Frank Stranahan came from a very wealthy family and played golf full-time. He was also one of the first players to realize that overall fitness was essential for golf and he went through a rigorous daily programme of weight training. He won the Amateur a second time in 1950 and twice finished second in the Open, most notably behind Hogan at Carnoustie in 1953. He was also runner-up in the US Masters as an amateur, but had relatively little success after he joined the professional ranks.

The man who followed him as next Amateur Champion at St Andrews also recognized the importance of keeping himself fit. The legendary Irishman Joe Carr started most mornings with a run and an hour's practice before going to the office, and a section of his local course was floodlit so that he could practise chipping and putting when work was over for the day.

But, despite the thousands of hours he spent on this department of the game, he was a notoriously fragile performer on the greens, finishing many a round by using a two-iron when he finally lost patience with the putter. His victory on the Old Course in 1958 was the second of the three Amateur titles he captured in a seven-year period. On the way to his St Andrews triumph he drove the green at the 316-yard twelfth and holed the putt for an eagle two. He was also a constant member of the Walker Cup team over eighteen years, but destined never to play on the winning side – an honour reserved for his son Roddy at St Andrews in 1971.

Another Walker Cup player, Michael Lunt, won the Amateur on the Old Course in 1963, and went on to create a family record three years later when he captured the English Amateur title – something which his father had also done 32 years before. Lunt was the last British player to win the Amateur at the Home of Golf. In 1976 John Davies missed a short putt on the first extra hole to give American Dick Siderowf the title for the second time and Frenchman Pierre Ploujoux used a marvellous putting touch on the huge double greens to gain his victory in 1981.

Post-war winners of the Amateur title at St Andrews included Joe Carr (CENTRE *and* LEFT) *in 1958 and* (RIGHT) *Michael Lunt, whose 1976 title was the last gained by a British player at the Home of Golf.*

For many years the international matches between the amateur players of Britain and America for the Walker Cup, first presented in 1922 by a relative of former President George Bush, were predictably one-sided. In the early years of the contest there was only one point between the teams when matches were played at St Andrews in 1923 and 1926, but in the next five contests the home side collected only six points out of a possible 60. The return to St Andrews in 1938 saw a welcome change in the pattern as Britain captured two of the foursomes encounters and added five singles victories for a three-point margin – and the first victory since the contest began.

There were some large scale wins in the 36-hole matches – Hector Thomson beating American Johnny Goodman by six and four and Gordon Peters taking care of Reynolds Smith by nine and eight. But by far the worst defeat was suffered by a member of the home team. Frank Pennink won the English Amateur title in both 1937 and 1938, but his one Walker Cup appearance finished on a very sour note. After winning his foursomes match in partnership with Leonard Crawley he suffered a 12 and 11 humiliation at the hands of Marvin Ward in the singles.

This was the last match played in the series before the Second World War and Pennink was given no chance to redeem himself when the contest restarted in 1947. He went on to become an accomplished golf administrator, writer, and course architect, and he was once the recipient of perhaps the most succinct telegram ever sent to a golf team. He was leading a British side in a contest in Scandinavia. After unpromising early results a message arrived from Gerald Micklem, then the Chairman of Selectors. It read simply: 'More snap – less schnapps'.

Back in St Andrews after the war, the Walker Cup returned to normal, with the United States team gaining a commanding victory – and it continued that way for the next three decades. Even a rematch over the Old Course in 1955 failed to halt the slide and Britain lost all the foursomes matches and gained only two points from the singles in a decidedly one-sided contest.

Bill Campbell, Captain of the US Walker Cup team, being presented with the trophy in 1955.

General Eisenhower visiting St Andrews. A notoriously keen golfer himself, Ike gave his name to the trophy for the World Amateur Team Championship which was first played for at St Andrews in 1958.

The signs were slightly more propitious when the match was again played over the Old Course in 1971. Two years earlier in Milwaukee, with the match now stretched to two series of foursomes and singles matches over two days, the home side had been given a clear warning as Britain came back strongly to close the gap to only two points at the end of play. Before the St Andrews encounter there were significant changes to the British selection policy. In previous years the British team had been chosen only a short while before the match. This time the side had been nominated at the end of the previous season, allowing players to work their way to peak form at the right time. Rodney Foster, who was to play in the matches five times and act as non-playing captain on two more occasions, summed up the shortcomings of the old system:

> Before the last home match, I sweated blood to get through the trials and into the
> team. Then I went through hell to prove I was playing well enough to be given a
> game. There was nothing left when the match started.

The whole team had more than enough left when the gun sounded at St Andrews: they created a sensation by taking all four points in the opening foursomes. But reality followed closely on the heels of euphoria as the Americans responded with tremendous fire-power in the afternoon singles. They entrusted the key matches to two young college students who were destined to make their mark in the professional game. Lanny Wadkins, a future USPGA winner, led from the front and US Open Champion-to-be Tom Kite brought up the rear as the United States team stormed back into the lead with six-and-a-half points from a possible eight. They went further ahead the next morning and set the home team a seemingly impossible task in the final series of singles matches.

99

The 1971 Walker cup saw the first British victory in 33 years. Captain of the British team was Michael Bonallack, pictured here with team member Warren Humphries.

The British had to win six matches out of eight to secure their first victory since the St Andrews triumph of 1938. Once again Wadkins and Kite did everything asked of them, capturing the points at the head and tail of the match. Four matches were decided on the final green, but the shot which ensured the return of the Walker Cup to Britain after a gap of 33 years was hit in the last match on the course by David Marsh – a searing long-iron to the seventeenth green to ensure that he was one-up playing the final hole.

It was entirely fitting that the decisive shot should have been hit by Marsh. A busy doctor with a practice in Southport, he was very much a weekend golfer, and he had a score to settle. He had been selected for the Walker Cup team once before, in 1959, but sat out the match without being given a game. Although entitled to wear his Walker Cup blazer he had steadfastly refused to do so until he played at St Andrews. That vital singles match was his last as a member of the team, but he was twice appointed non-playing captain.

The isolated British victory was a bitter-sweet experience for team captain Michael Bonallack, who gained only one point from four matches. 'At a time when I wanted to play the best golf of my life I played my worst,' he said. 'My team won despite their captain.' As the present-day Secretary of the Royal and Ancient Golf Club, with an office that overlooks the expanse of the first and eighteenth fairways of the Old Course, he occasionally still reflects on the dramatic events of a week in which the tide was fleetingly turned.

Perhaps in the hope that the setting of St Andrews would inspire the home team to recapture the winning ways of 1938 and 1971, the next home match was again played on the Old Course, but a dominant American team once again returned home with the trophy. A young newcomer to that team, Curtis Strange, took an instant liking to the atmosphere of St Andrews and won three-and-a-half points from four matches. Twelve years later he was to set a new record of 62 for the Old Course, and he went on to win the US Open two years in a row.

A host of amateur team events have been played at St Andrews in addition to the Walker Cup, ranging from Boys' Internationals, Commonwealth Tournaments, European Team Championships and St Andrews Trophy contests between Britain and Europe, to the inaugural World Amateur Team Championship for the Eisenhower Trophy in 1958. This last is a contest which features four-man teams from the world's golfing nations, with the best three rounds to count each day over four days. Unbelievably the first contest finished with Australia and the United States tied on 918, Australia winning the play-off by just two shots.

The British Ladies Championship, which started in 1893, was not played at St Andrews until 1908, but is best remembered for the 1929 confrontation between the best women golfers from Britain and America. Glenna Collett was the American sensation: winner of the US, Canadian and French Championships, at the age of 18 she had hit a measured drive of over 300 yards. In the 36-hole final at St Andrews she faced Joyce Wethered, who had retired from competitive golf some four years earlier after winning the title three times in four seasons.

Wethered had come out of retirement because the Championship was being played on the Old Course and she wanted the opportunity to win at the Home of Golf. Her chances looked slim after the opening nine holes which Collett played in 34 to be five up, but by lunch she had cut the deficit to two. In an inspired afternoon spell she won six of the first nine holes, but Collett fought back and as they stood on the sixteenth green the margin had been cut to two.

In those days the railway line to St Andrews ran through the heart of the links and Wethered astounded her opponent and the large gallery of spectators by holing a difficult putt to maintain her lead as a train rumbled by only a few feet from the edge of the green. She won the match on the next green and as she walked up the final fairway a close friend asked why she had putted while the train was passing. 'What train?' she asked.

Joyce Wethered, who won her fourth British Ladies title at St Andrews in 1929 after an epic contest with the American Champion, Glenna Collett.

The intense level of concentration Wethered gave to the game had allowed her to blot out the existence of the distraction, but it was also one of the reasons why she had given up competitive play a few years before. Within minutes of her St Andrews victory she fainted.

Similarly light-headed feelings overtook two members of the R & A when the Ladies Championship was last played on the Old Course in 1975. The strictly male precincts of the clubhouse were opened up to competitors for the duration of the event – and two reactionary stalwarts resigned. Not all the dramatic moments in St Andrews are confined to the golf course.

Chapter 8

Sons of
St Andrews

S T ANDREWS' LEGACIES to the game of golf include not only the world's oldest
surviving course and its most famous club, but also some of the greatest characters in
the annals of golfing history. It is the memory of these men and their contributions to
the sport which, every bit as much as the sacred turf of the Old Course or the hallowed por-
tals of the Royal and Ancient, continue to draw visitors to the Home of Golf.

The very first player to be recognized as a true professional was Allan Robertson. Born
into a golfing family in St Andrews in 1815, he scampered around the links as a youngster,
watching and learning from the leading players. Short and thick-set, he developed a rhythmic swing which relied on perfect timing, in great contrast to the majority of golfers of his
day who lashed into the ball with aggressive actions that almost spun them off their feet.
Good judges of the golf swing who lived long enough to see both Robertson and Harry
Vardon play the game were aware of a great similarity in their style of play – and Vardon
became known as the father of the modern swing.

Robertson's prowess as a player was legendary, though few recorded facts survive to give
hard evidence of his ability. But there are strong reasons to believe that he would have left a
telling record in the annals of the Open Championship had he not died of jaundice two
years before the event was first played in 1860. He certainly formed a formidable partnership with Old Tom Morris, who was, in fact, six years his junior. There is no evidence that
they were ever beaten in foursomes matches. Claims that Robertson was also unbeaten in
singles are opposed by other accounts which say he avoided such matches after an early loss.
This seems highly unlikely in the light of the records of the R & A for 1842. It had become
the custom at the end of the club's autumn meeting for the members to contribute funds –
known as in-puts – to be played for by the caddies. The club minutes record the fact that
these were won by Tom Morris with a round of 92. Although he was later to become uni-
versally known as Old Tom, he was then only 21 and it was his father who took second place
on 99. But the significant part of the report continued:

*Allan Robertson, the
first recognized
professional and the
finest golfer of his day.*

103

Allan Robertson was prohibited by his brethren for competing for these stakes on account of his superior play, it being their impression that they would have no chance in any contest in which Allan took part.

He was then 27 years of age. There must have been many times in the modern game when their fellow professionals would have welcomed such a prohibition against Jack Nicklaus or Seve Ballesteros.

Robertson was not only the finest golfer of his day, he was also an expert maker of featherie balls and Old Tom Morris was employed as his assistant in this arduous business. A good ball-maker produced on average no more than four in a day and the price was correspondingly high. Robertson therefore had good reason to suppose that his livelihood was under threat when the much cheaper gutta percha ball was introduced in about 1848. Determined to stop the spread of the new ball, he paid school children to bring him any gutties they could find so that he could burn them.

Robertson must have known that he was fighting a losing battle, and the situation was not helped when he saw Tom Morris using one of the new balls. Morris' action was not a deliberate affront to his employer's wishes, he was playing the Old Course with a Mr Campbell and, having split the last of his featherie balls, was offered a guttie to try. But when he passed his boss on the course Tom knew trouble was brewing. He described the encounter later:

> I could see fine from the expression on his face that he did not like it at all, and, when we met afterwards in his shop, we had high words about the matter, and there and then we parted company, I leaving his employment.

Robertson was eventually forced to move with the times and switched to the easier and faster production of the new balls. He lived out the last years of his life in a small, white-painted cottage overlooking the sea from the hill behind the R & A clubhouse, walking briskly down to the first tee whenever called upon to teach or play with the members, and always wearing a red coat. The few photographs which exist show him with a rather gloomy, dour countenance, but he was remembered by all who knew him as a kind and lively person. A memorial marks his grave in St Andrews cathedral cemetery.

Shortly after Old Tom Morris parted company from Allan Robertson he was tempted away from St Andrews to become Keeper of the Green at Prestwick. He was there when the Open Championship was created by the members of the club and, although he failed to win the inaugural event in 1860, he had captured the title three times before 1864. In that year he brought his family back to St Andrews where he was employed as a professional golfer by the R & A at a salary of £50 a year:

TOP *Old Tom Morris in action.*
BELOW *A group of nineteenth-century St Andrews stalwarts, including Old Tom Morris (second from left) and Allan Robertson (third from right).*

On the understanding that he shall have entire charge of the golf course and be responsible for it being kept in proper order, and that he shall be the servant of the Club under the direction and control of the committee in charge of the green.

He was to incur the displeasure of that committee on more than one occasion.

Morris returned to Prestwick to win the Open Championship for the fourth and last time in 1867, after which his son, Young Tom, took over and began his own domination of the event. Old Tom survived until he was 86 and one of the reasons he put forward for his long and active life was that he took a dip in the sea every day. A visitor at Prestwick once called for help for a man on the beach 'trying hard to drown himself'. He was assured it was only Old Tom breaking the ice for his morning swim.

He continued to play an excellent game of golf throughout his life, scoring 82 round the Old Course when he was 80 years old. How many more Championships he could have won in his prime if he had been blessed with the putting stroke of his son is impossible to tell. It was a problem that plagued him throughout his playing career. Young Tom once remarked that his father would be a great putter if the hole was always a yard closer. So famous did he become for missing from close range that a letter addressed simply to 'The Misser of Short Putts, Prestwick' was delivered to his door without delay.

Long after his competitive playing days were over Old Tom was actively involved in golf course design. In reply to an enquiry in 1894 about his charges, he wrote: 'My fee for laying out a green is £1 per day and travelling expenses.' He had an expert eye for terrain and was always able to get the most from the natural contours, an important factor in an age when large-scale earth-moving was not a practical proposition. He was the first designer to plan courses with double loops coming back to the clubhouse, not so much for the convenience of golfers as to achieve a greater variety of shots.

Although he was a man who earned great respect as a golfer, he was also a strong-willed individual who said and did what he thought was right. This brought him into conflict with his employers, the Greens Committee of the R & A, in 1895. As soon as that year's Open Championship was completed he removed the flagsticks from the greens and filled the holes with sand. In his opinion the course needed a rest. A notice was published immediately in the town which read:

> This Committee, learning that the golf holes on the Old Course have been filled up by the Custodian of the Links without authority, regret if any inconvenience should have been caused to the Public, and that such action should have been taken without notice and general agreement among golfers, but recognising that the Old Course is much in need of rest, resolve to allow the holes to remain closed until 30 June.

Old Tom had got away with his high-handed action, but one member of the Greens Committee, A.F. Macfie, the first winner of the Amateur Championship, had already tired of his autocratic behaviour some two years earlier. In offering his resignation he wrote:

> I must decline to serve as long as the green committee is a mere collective puppet in Tom Morris's hands. I think it is a perfect farce having one at all: and till a green committee would be supported by the general feeling of the Club in any dispute with Morris – which is far from being the case at present – there is no earthly use in trying to improve the course in any way.

Yet in 1896 a testimonial to provide for Morris' old age raised £1,240, a considerable sum at the time, from golfers around the world; and when it became time for Old Tom to retire at the age of 82 in 1903 his relationship with the R & A was such that they continued to pay his salary. He was still in excellent health on the day in May 1908 when, after enjoying a few drams of whisky in the New Club, he mistook the door leading to the cellar for the entrance to the toilet and fell heavily into the basement. He died shortly afterwards in the local hospital.

On the day of his funeral no golf was played in St Andrews as golfers throughout the world mourned the end of a long and rich life, yet one which was touched by personal tragedy – for he had outlived his wife, his daughter and all three of his sons.

The most talented member of Old Tom's family had been Tommy – Young Tom as he was later called. Born just before his father left St Andrews to take up his appointment at Prestwick, he grew up on the west coast links and showed prodigious talent for the game at an early age, beating a field of leading professionals while only 13.

In 1868 he succeeded his father as Open Champion at the age of 17 and kept the title in the following two years. After his third victory, under the original rules of the Championship, he retained the belt awarded each year to the winner. In his third successive victory he was no less than 12 strokes ahead of his nearest rival over 36 holes with a total of 149, incredible scoring given the condition of the course and the equipment in use. He won

'Young Tom Morris' last match', 1875.

again when the Championship was resumed in 1872 and that year set a new low score of 77 for the Old Course, bettering Allan Robertson's long-standing record by two shots.

He was the first professional who made his living entirely from playing the game. He was never attached to a club as caddie-master or green-keeper and did not make clubs and balls for sale. Instead he played money matches and took part in open events. In 1874 he added to his income by winning a wager that he would play the Old Course every day for a week in 82 strokes or less. He married in November of that year and his father entertained his workmen and a few friends at supper. After the normal toast to bride and groom, the *Fifeshire Journal* reported, 'The usual shop toast – Long may the Hammer strike and the Lathe Turn – brought the proceedings of a very agreeable evening to a close.'

It was less than a year later, while Tommy and his father were playing in a great money match at North Berwick, that a telegram arrived addressed to Old Tom. He told his son only that they had to leave at once to return home, and a wealthy patron put his yacht at their disposal to sail directly across the Firth of Forth, a considerably quicker route than the tedious rail journey through Edinburgh.

It was only as they pulled into the harbour at St Andrews that Old Tom broke the news to his son that his young bride had died in childbirth together with their baby. A St Andrews minister, Dr Boyd, was in the house when they arrived and wrote later:

> I never forgot the young man's stony look – stricken was the word – and how all of a sudden he started up and cried – 'It's not true'. I have seen many sorrowful things, but not many like that Saturday night.

Young Tom played golf only twice after his wife's death, and then solely because the matches had been arranged long in advance. The romantic story has it that he died of a broken heart, and certainly he suffered from severe depression. But he also failed to eat properly and took to bouts of lonely drinking. His father found him dead on Christmas morning of that same year. An artery in his lung had burst. The greatest champion of his age was just 24 years old.

A public subscription paid for a memorial which still stands above his grave in the cathedral cemetery.

Young Tom's memorial in the cemetery of St Andrews Cathedral.

It was almost thirty years after the death of Young Tom that, following the death of his father, Andrew Kirkaldy was elevated to the position of professional to the R & A. Kirkaldy had finished second in the Open of 1879 at the age of 19 and was runner-up again two years later. After service with the Black Watch at Omdurman and Tel-el-Kebir he returned to tie for the Championship with Willie Park at Musselburgh in 1889, but lost the play-off. Two years later he played second fiddle to his young brother Hugh over the Old Course, this time finishing in a tie for second place.

He was probably the best St Andrews golfer never to win the Open, and if certain members of the R & A felt they had had problems with the forth-right straight-talking of Tom Morris, they certainly gained no respite from the tongue of Andrew Kirkaldy. On one occasion, he was carrying for a prominent member of the club whose golfing ambitions, on that day at least, were far in advance of his ability. A succession of disasters culminated with the unfortunate golfer's ball finally plummeting into the depths of the Road Hole bunker. 'What do I take out of here?' came the anguished cry. Kirkaldy's advice, pithily phrased, was to try the 2.40 train to Edinburgh.

He managed to upset the entire membership of the Honourable Company of Edinburgh Golfers when they opened their new course at Muirfield in 1892 by describing it as: 'Nothing but an old water meadow' and even men of the cloth were not protected from his quick tongue. Not used to being challenged over his advice on playing the Old Course, Kirkaldy was somewhat taken aback when a bishop whose clubs he was carrying insisted on using his mashie from Hell bunker when the wise old professional had handed him the niblick, a much more lofted club and better suited to the task. But the bishop was not to be moved and proceeded to hit the shot of a lifetime on to the green. As he emerged from the sand with a self-satisfied smile on his face Kirkaldy gave him a withering look and commented: 'When you die, mind and tak that club wi' ye.'

Yet such was his strength of character and knowledge of the game that he gained the often grudging respect of members and visitors, and in many cases their lasting friendship.

ABOVE *Andrew Kirkaldy, Old Tom's successor as the R & A professional, outside the clubhouse in the 1920s, and* (BELOW) *with the Prince of Wales, later King Edward VIII, in 1930.*

Willie Auchterlonie succeeded Andrew Kirkaldy as R & A Professional in 1934. In his youth (ABOVE LEFT) he had won the 1893 Open, using just seven clubs, which he still treasured over sixty years later (BELOW). Like his son Laurie (TOP RIGHT) he was also a celebrated clubmaker.

On Kirkaldy's death in 1934 his position with the R & A was filled by a very different character. Willie Auchterlonie had won the Open in 1893 at the age of 21, playing with a set of seven clubs which he had made himself. He only used five of them over the 72 holes at Prestwick.

He continued to play in the championships for a few years but most of his time and effort were spent in building up the famous clubmaking company of D. & W. Auchterlonie. He was a quiet man, constantly seeking perfection from himself and his clubmakers and very slow to offer praise. By this time, of course, professionals no longer acted as caddies and the relationship between the R & A's honorary professional and the members was consequently a more distant one.

He was succeeded in the position by his son Laurie, who, by his own admission did not have the right temperament for competitive golf, although he played the game to a high standard. Instead he specialized in clubmaking. Even when the family business closed in the era of mass production, he continued to produce, from a small workshop close to the eighteenth green of the Old Course, a few highly prized and beautifully crafted clubs for privileged clients and friends. Also an avid collector of antique clubs, he created his own small museum, the bulk of his collection being gifted to the R & A on his death. The next professional, the first non-St Andrean appointed to the post, was John Panton, a former conqueror of Sam Snead for the World Senior Championship and a Scottish Ryder Cup and World Cup player, who holds the position to this day.

Willie Auchterlonie, Open Champion of 1893, greets Gary Player, who won the title in 1959.

Bobby Jones, the young American golfing genius who gained a permanent place in the hearts of St Andreans.

Although St Andrews has always given its first loyalty to its native sons, it has also found a place in its civic heart for a select few of those many champions from foreign lands who have come to test their skills against the Old Course. Of these, none have had such an impact on the old, grey city as Bobby Jones, who, over a period of no more than a handful of years, became an adopted son of St Andrews. Jones was only 19 when he first arrived to take part in the 1921 Open, but his reputation had travelled ahead of him. Although he had yet to win a major event, the story of the sickly young boy emerging as a potential world-beater had captured the public imagination – nowhere more so than at the Home of Golf.

Not long after the birth of their child his parents determined to try to improve the health of their ailing son. They moved out of the city of Atlanta in the southern state of Georgia to a house overlooking the East Lakes golf course in the suburbs and virtually put him out to grass – encouraging him to spend his days outdoors without shoes. A neighbour's gift of a cut-down hickory club and three less than perfect golf balls got him started in the game. He created his own five-hole course, four in the garden of the house and a long one of 60 yards along the rutted lane outside. Only two rules were involved in his games with other local kids – the ball was played wherever it lay and every stroke or attempted stroke was counted.

By the age of six both his health and his golf were blossoming and he spent hours trailing around the East Lakes course in the wake of the taciturn Scot, Stewart Maiden, who had arrived from Carnoustie to take over the professional's post from his brother Jimmy. Crucially, it was Maiden's swing that Jones copied.

He broke 80 for the first time when he was 11. Three years later he was Georgia State Champion and had won through two rounds in the US Amateur. By the time he was 17 he had reached the finals of the US and Canadian Amateur Championships and at 20 was runner-up in the US Open. Nothing, it seemed, could stop the progress of this charismatic young man. But Jones was to admit later that his biggest battles were with himself. He had a fiery temper and was well known for his club-throwing antics as a youngster. Every match became a battle on two fronts: against his opponent and against his own temperament. The struggle often left him mentally and physically exhausted.

He was never to lose that inner turmoil, but at St Andrews in 1921 he learned to control it. After dropping more than a dozen shots by the time he reached the short eleventh hole in the third round of that year's Open he picked up his ball and withdrew from the contest. It was the only time in his life that he failed to complete a championship and the shame he felt at this behaviour at the very Home of Golf sparked in him the determination to exercise iron control over his emotions from that moment on.

Once he had won this battle with himself, Jones' staggering ability as a player was unleashed. In a seven-year period he won 13 national titles, culminating in the capture of the US and British Open and Amateur Championships in one incredible season in 1930. Then, at the age of 28, he retired from competitive golf. Fittingly, a part of that 1930 triumph was achieved at St Andrews, where he won the Amateur title on a course that he first hated and then came to love, and although his golf career came to a sudden end that summer his links with St Andrews were to grow ever stronger.

Back home in Georgia he continued his career as a lawyer, but also played a leading part in creating the Augusta National Golf Club and the annual Masters Championship. The fourth hole at Augusta is his tribute to St Andrews – the fiercely sloped green and severe bunkers to

left and right a direct copy of the eleventh hole of the Old Course where his metamorphosis from raw amateur to seasoned champion began.

Jones was to play the Old Course just one more time. On his way to watch the Berlin Olympics of 1936 he stopped over at Gleneagles and could not bear to be so close to St Andrews without playing. There is a bush telegraph in the old city second to none and by the time he arrived on the first tee a crowd of some 5,000 had gathered to welcome him. The gallery continued to grow as the round progressed and shopkeepers put up their closed signs so that they could see their hero play. It was worth the loss of earnings, for although Jones had been playing little golf he reached the turn in 32 and completed the round under par.

If that visit brought a gleam to thousands of eyes, his next and final journey to St Andrews filled them with tears. The first World Amateur Team Championship for the Eisenhower Trophy was played over the Old Course in October 1958 and Jones, a close friend of General Eisenhower, had accepted the captaincy of the American team. He was by this time suffering from a crippling spinal disease and arrived by golf buggy to receive an honour seldom bestowed in the ancient city. He became only the second American to be made a Freeman of the Burgh of St Andrews. The first was Benjamin Franklin. He spoke of his growing admiration for the links:

The more I studied the Old Course, the more I loved it and the more I loved it the more I studied it, so that I came to feel that it was for me the most favourable meeting ground possible for an important contest.

I felt that my knowledge of the course enabled me to play it with patience and restraint until she might exact her toll from my adversary, who might treat her with less respect and understanding.

I could take out of my life everything except my experiences at St Andrews and I would still have had a rich and full life.

He spoke also of friendship:

When I say to a person 'I am your friend,' I have said about the ultimate. When I say 'You are my friend,' I am assuming too much.

But when I have said as much about you and you have done so much for me, I think that when I say 'You are my friends,' then, under these circumstances, I am at the same time affirming my affection and regard for you and expressing my complete faith in you and my trust in the sincerity of your friendship.

Therefore, when I say now to you 'Greetings, my friends at St Andrews', I know I am not presuming, because of what has passed between us.

As he walked painfully back to his golf buggy and moved down the aisle to the door, the words of the old Scots song 'Will Ye No Come Back Again?' started as a low whisper and then rose to a crescendo as every voice joined in. Then he was gone, and throats which had sung so lustily were suddenly incapable of speech. Bobby Jones was never able to respond to the invitation in the song before he died in 1971. The tenth hole of the Old Course was named in his memory a year later.

No other player could hope to fill the place of Bobby Jones in the hearts of St Andreans, but the city was soon to extend its deep respect to a young Australian player, Peter Thomson, who became a specialist on the Old Course and who, in recent years, has made a very practical contribution to the city's attractions.

Thomson was something of an enigma. He had wide-ranging interests outside the game and liked to get away from the course and from all talk of golf once the day's work had been successfully completed. He had learned his golf at a small club in Melbourne, taking it seriously from the age of 13. Pictures of St Andrews around the clubhouse walls whetted his appetite for a visit to the Home of Golf and left him in no doubt that, in golf, everything came out of St Andrews. When he finally arrived, to take part in the Match-play Championship of 1954, he was not disappointed. 'It was just the way I had imagined it,' he said later. 'It was September and there was a marvellous soft light. I thought I had found a bit of heaven.'

He had already shown his liking for links golf by winning the Open at Birkdale two months earlier and it did not take him long to convert his enthusiasm for the Old Course into the ability to master its ancient challenge. His first taste of St Andrews ended in victory.

Within a year he was back for the Open Championship. The course was very different from the one he had encountered the previous September, much drier and faster and swept by strong winds. Yet his victory seemed assured until near-disaster struck at the long fourteenth in the final round. Being a little too careful to avoid the wall on the right, he drove into the group of bunkers known as the Beardies. With his ball lying close up under the face he had to play out backwards. His next shot safely cleared Hell bunker, but ran on into another small trap close to the green. For the second time on the same hole he had to turn his back on the green and play away from the hole. The result was a rather unpleasant seven which virtually wiped out his lead. But he recovered immediately with a birdie at the next hole and remembers 'coming home carefully from there'.

He was to finish second to his great rival Bobby Locke when the Open returned to St Andrews only two years later, but he gained his third victory over the Old Course in the Martini International of 1962. He feels that many of the terrors of links golf have been diminished as courses become softer and more watered and that developments in the design and construction of the golf ball have given the professionals a far greater degree of control. He remembers Henry Cotton telling him how dry and difficult the Old Course had been in the Open of 1939. It had been impossible to stop the ball on the first green by playing it straight on. The only solution was to hit the drive far to the left by the Swilcan Bridge and play into the green sideways, using its width to work the ball close to a pin position near the burn.

In recent years, Thomson's rapport with St Andrews has grown even closer than it was in the days when he was winning titles over the Old Course. He has been a regular visitor in the 90s, designing a fine new course on high ground behind the ancient city. 'When you play in the championships you are more or less divorced from everything around you,' he explained. 'Now I feel I am beginning to understand and enjoy the community a lot more.'

The new course – which belongs to the Old Course Hotel – looks down over the city and St Andrews Bay with distant views to the Grampian Mountains. At well over 7,000 yards and winding through trees, burns and gorse, it is designed to last into the future. 'I hope St Andrews will be proud of it,' says Thomson of the creation which has given him the opportunity to add a new dimension to the challenge of the Home of Golf some four decades after he first fell under its spell.

Peter Thomson with the Open Championship trophy he won in 1955 at St Andrews. Thomson won over the Old Course on two other occasions, the Match-play Championship of 1954 and the Martini International in 1962.

OVERLEAF. The new Craigtoun Course, designed by Peter Thomson in the 1990s.

115

Arnold Palmer. Although he never won a St Andrews Open, his visit in 1960 marked a turning point for the Championship and also launched a lifelong partnership with St Andrews caddie 'Tip' Anderson.

Arnold Palmer's flirtation with the Old Course lasted exactly 30 years, but still failed to give him the championship success he craved at the birthplace of the game. American interest in the Open Championship had waned throughout the 50s, but the arrival of Palmer, newly crowned as US Open Champion, for the Centenary Open at St Andrews in 1960, was to prove a dramatic turning point; the television coverage of that Championship marked the point at which golf began to gain a mass audience among British viewers. Palmer's interest in the Open continued long after he had any chance of winning, and his leadership and enthusiasm inspired a new generation of American professionals to regard the world's oldest championship as one of the key fixtures in the professional calendar.

Palmer's participation in the Centenary Open also launched one of the great partnerships in the game's history, throwing together a young St Andrews caddie and the game's rising superstar. Jimmy Anderson – known throughout the world of golf as Tip – soon proved to Palmer that his knowledge of the Old Course was encyclopaedic. A four-handicap player in his own right, he had played and studied the course for years. He convinced Palmer that the general advice to drive left – that the Old was a hooker's course – was completely wrong. He had pinpointed 16 exact areas into which the ball had to be driven to leave second shots that avoided bunkers and mounds.

Palmer was to finish the week in second spot, one shot behind Kel Nagle. His putting had been uncharacteristically poor and three putts on the final green in the third round almost brought the budding relationship with Anderson to an abrupt halt. After Palmer had driven over the road at the last hole, Anderson suggested a big wedge for the approach shot. The ball hit the front of the green and rolled back, from where Palmer took three more. 'That was the wrong club,' he snapped. Later that afternoon in his hotel room overlooking the eighteenth hole, Palmer told Anderson he still thought he was wrong. Anderson took him to the window and pointed out that anyone who hit the ball as far as Palmer could hit a wedge shot 90 yards. The American surveyed the scene, looked his caddie in the eye and said, with a smile: 'That looks right enough.' The next moment he was loading Anderson with gifts of shirts and sweaters and has never since played in Britain without Tip carrying the bag.

Anderson had the chance to travel with Palmer in America, but chose to remain based in the home of golf. And, although their first outing together in Britain had not culminated in an Open title, Anderson did help Palmer to capture the next two Championships: he won by a single shot at Royal Birkdale and by a staggering six shots at Troon in 1962. Palmer's major victories were all achieved within the space of six years and he was never again to mount a sustained challenge in the Open. But he continued to play year after year, finally announcing his retirement from the Championship in the 1990 event back where it had all started 30 years before – at St Andrews. Accompanied by a not-so-young Tip Anderson he completed the first two rounds in level par, good enough to have qualified for the final stages at every Open over that span of three decades – but sadly one too many on his farewell appearance. As he hit a masterful running shot close to the hole on the final green the thousands of loyal supporters packed into the huge grandstands rose as one to bid farewell to a man who had graced the Open Championship and St Andrews golf for so long.

The American challenge which Palmer had relaunched with his entry into the Open in 1960 was to be continued by the player who dethroned him. Jack Nicklaus had learned his golf in America on a course designed by Scotsman Donald Ross, a one-time assistant to Old Tom Morris at St Andrews. 'I always enjoyed playing the old courses and was a very traditional person in that way', he recalls. Adding the Open Championship to his growing list of conquests had always been one of his overriding ambitions.

His first opportunity at St Andrews came in 1964, when despite closing rounds of 66 and 68, he failed to catch the runaway Tony Lema by five shots. But what he did succeed in eliciting was a warm and genuine reception from the Scottish galleries, something which had been singularly lacking in his home country. There he was seen as the young upstart who was stealing titles from the folk hero Arnold Palmer. In St Andrews his outstanding ability and his obvious respect for the Old Course and the traditions of the ancient game were the only yardsticks that mattered.

By the time the Open returned in 1970 Nicklaus had already won at Muirfield, his eighth major title after successes in the US Open, Masters and PGA Championships. But three years had gone by without an addition to the list. Had he burned himself out? Arriving a week in advance of the championship he went through a planned routine of practice and play, shutting himself off from the distractions that surround the major events. Yet at the end of the fourth round he felt that the title had eluded him once again. Then fellow American Doug Sanders had a short downhill, left-to-right putt for victory – and missed.

*Past Open Champions –
St Andrews 1970.*

A great sportsman. Jack Nicklaus after receiving an honorary degree from St Andrews University in 1984.

Nicklaus was reprieved and the following day stood over a 7-foot putt on the Tom Morris green that would make him the champion at the Home of Golf. It hesitated agonizingly on the lip before falling and Nicklaus' ambition was achieved.

Nicklaus was to win again at St Andrews, in far less dramatic circumstances, in 1978, and six years later was awarded an honorary degree at St Andrews University. At the ceremony his unfailing sportsmanship was recalled, exemplified by the putt which he conceded to Tony Jacklin on the final green of their Ryder Cup match at Royal Birkdale in 1969. 'I wouldn't want you to lose by missing that', said Nicklaus, in a gesture which ensured that the entire match finished all-square, and which earned him the displeasure of his team captain, Sam Snead.

Nicklaus also shared the sense of compassion which the whole of St Andrews felt for Doug Sanders over that infamous putt which had given the Golden Bear victory in 1970. Sanders had been forced to fight his way through the qualifying rounds for that year's Open and had stood within 3 feet of outright victory before it was snatched from his grasp. A tough and colourful character from Georgia, he has earned a rightful place in Old Course history. Talking many years later of the fateful moment, he consoled himself with the knowledge that his name was now synonymous with St Andrews. Did he still think about the missed putt. 'Yes,' he replied, 'but only once every ten minutes.'

The latest of the Championship winners at St Andrews – Seve Ballesteros, who gave a typically charging performance in 1984, and Nick Faldo, who earned his title with a week of inspired precision golf in 1990 – will undoubtedly continue to write their own chapters in the annals of St Andrews. Their names will join the long and distinguished list of those who have helped shape the history of the old city and will, in turn, be joined by future champions as yet unborn.

Chapter 9

THE CADDIES

CADDIES, A MUCH MALIGNED and fast disappearing race, were, in fact, the original golf professionals – specifically invited by Lord Colville in October 1860 to take part in the very first Open Championship at Prestwick. A letter sent out to the leading clubs stated that: 'Competitors must be known, honest and respectable caddies.'

Yet so slim were the rewards in the early Championships that the winners would go back to carrying clubs after their brief moment of glory. For most, caddying was a poorly paid and precarious existence, although preferable, for those with less than Calvinistic work ethics, to a regular shift in a coalmine or twelve hours a day at a forge. They had a certain amount of freedom and worked in the fresh air, the majority were also keen and competent golfers. Many of the St Andrews caddies were fishermen. The good golfers among them would supplement their income by carrying clubs when the fishing was poor or the weather too bad to venture out. They called their secondary employment 'grass-hopping'.

But not all caddies were part-timers. Indeed, the leading players in the early days of organized club and society golf invariably came from the ranks of the caddies. These men often formed lasting partnerships with wealthy golfers and it was not unknown for genuine and lifelong friendships to develop between men from totally different classes and backgrounds. Sadly, as the game was taken up by the English middle and upper classes such relationships became less common. In Scotland, golf had been a game of the people. It took the false values of the English class system to turn it into a symbol of elitism – a millstone which it still struggles to throw off in some of that country's more stagnant social backwaters.

The first professionals in Scotland would often form close and lasting friendships with wealthy landowners and noblemen. They shared golf, good food and drink. Old Tom Morris was able to sit in the R & A clubhouse and engage in deep conversation with a British Prime Minister. Yet, in England, by the turn of the century professionals were treated very much as second-class citizens. They were club servants who made and repaired clubs, gave lessons and played with members – but were not allowed to set foot in the clubhouse. Unfortunately, it was also these same Victorian empire builders who took the game to so many different parts of the world, establishing it as a sport full of crass snobbishness and suffocating arrogance far removed from its true roots.

Caddies who found a permanent post with a single employer might spend one day carrying the clubs for their employers and the next play in partnership with them in high-stakes foursomes matches. They would also be expected to clean and repair the clubs and coach their masters in the finer arts of the game. Old Tom Morris' brother George, for example, was given full-time employment by Robert Chambers of the encyclopaedia publishing family, to whom he acted as general handyman, caddie and playing partner.

Those who were less highly regarded might carry the clubs on a regular basis for an individual or a group of golfers. A typical example was Lang Willie, a St Andrews caddie of some notoriety. He found himself regular work carrying for lecturers from the university, but was not impressed with their ability. 'Learning Latin and Greek is all very fine,' he explained, 'but you need brains to be a golfer.'

Dressed always in a tall hat and tail coat, whether on or off the course, Lang Willie insisted that he drank nothing but sweet milk. Yet it is doubtful if such an innocent brew could have been solely responsible for reducing him almost nightly to a state of semi-consciousness. His strange clothing was almost certainly a gift from a grateful golfer and it was commonplace for cast-off garments to be handed down from player to caddie in this way. As a result it was sometimes difficult at distance to tell rich from poor on the links. Closer, but not too close, inspection would quickly reveal which was wearing the ill-fitting and dirty clothes.

Cleanliness and sobriety were not high on the list of priorities for many caddies and at Prestwick there were complaints about their filthy condition. It was decided that they should be inspected and the 'very unclean' not allowed to carry. Such close inspection of Willie Gunn in the early 1800s would have been a singularly unrewarding experience. When he left his home in the Highlands each spring to work as a caddie further south he would put on every stitch of clothing he owned – three pairs of trousers, several shirts and as many as four coats, the inner ones with their sleeves cut off. Any gifts of clothing from golfers were simply added on top and he never appeared to remove any before making the trek home in winter.

A century later, a local caddie in St Andrews, comparatively well-dressed, explained to a visiting golfer that he had carried for, and was a close acquaintance of, Britain's Prime Minister, A.J. Balfour. Knowing that an unyielding attachment to the truth was not a common characteristic of caddies at the time – although their present-day counterparts are absolutely blameless in this respect – the visitor pressed for further details of the caddie's association with the great man. 'I'm wearing a pair of his trousers,' came the reply.

It was, perhaps, only common justice that golfers should pass on their cast-off clothing, for caddie-fees were not generous and players were actively discouraged from over-stepping the mark. In June 1771 the Society of St Andrews Golfers entered in their minute book the following resolution:

Fred Buchanan's postcard, published in about 1906, was probably one of a set and illustrates the high cost of ignoring one's caddie's advice in the days of hickory-shafted clubs.

"WULL YE TAK MA ADVICE NOO?"

The Captain and Company agree and appoint that in time coming the Caddies who carry the Clubs or run before the Players, or are otherwise engaged by the Gentlemen Golfers, are to get four pence for going the length of the holl called the Holl o' Cross and if they go further than that they are to get six pence and no more.

Any of the Gentlemen of this Society transgressing this rule are to pay two pint bottles of claret at the first meeting they shall attend.

The caddies who ran before the players, specifically mentioned in these early records of the Society which was later to become the Royal and Ancient, were an essential part of the game. There were blind shots on every course in those days. In fact, they were considered the more challenging and sporting holes. In order that the expensive featherie balls which were in use at the time should not be lost, a fore-caddie would run ahead of each match, and on some notoriously difficult holes a young caddie would be permanently stationed in all weathers so that he could indicate to players whether balls had finished in or out of bounds. An elaborate system of signalling was also devised so that golfers could know instantly if their shot had finished in the fairway or if it was in the rough, and whether it was in a good or bad lie. Bob Ferguson, who won three Open Championships in a row from 1880, had been a fore-caddie in his young days. He explained:

They were very impatient these old golfers, and as there was nearly always a wager on the match, you could not let them know too soon what their chances were of winning or losing the hole.

LEFT *Preparing for a round in the 1950s.* ABOVE *Caddies await their players outside the starter's hut in the early 1900s; note that the caddie on the left still prefers to carry the clubs, bag and all, beneath his arm in the fashion of an earlier age.*

By the very nature of their job, these youngsters who ran before the players were under constant bombardment and warning shouts of 'Fore-caddie!' would regularly ring out over the links. Inevitably and very quickly this was shortened to the cry of 'Fore!' which reverberates around the courses of the world to this day.

Despite the dangers of always being in front of the golfers, the fore-caddies had excellent opportunities to supplement their meagre income. It was quite common for the caddies, as well as the golfers, to bet on the outcome of matches. Being, quite literally, ahead of the game, the fore-caddies had ample opportunity to nudge one ball into a good lie or kick another into the rough. Many a hole-in-one – and the large tip which comes in its wake – was achieved at blind holes by means of a caddie's boot.

There was also a simple means of improving upon the normal fee by 'losing' a ball on the links. Although such carelessness would result in immediate loss of half of the sixpence the caddie would normally have received, the ball could be sold later for nine pence. A favoured technique was to step on a ball in the rough while the players and other caddies were preoccupied with the search. Once the ball was well buried the caddie would drop a scrap of rag or a twig to mark the exact spot and come back after the round to retrieve the ball from its grave and thus liberate a few additional pennies.

RIGHT The winning caddie collects the traditional golden sovereign after retrieving the ball with which the incoming captain of the R & A drives himself into office.
BELOW How the Ginger Beer hole got its name. Retired caddie Daw Anderson provides refreshment to a thirsty golfer.

At the first hole on the Old Course any balls which finished in the Swilcan Burn could be hidden from view by an alert caddie rushing forward and stirring up the mud and sand to cloud the water, all the time making out that he was raking around in the murky depths in search of the errant ball. As the match moved down the second hole an accomplice would wait patiently by the burn for the mud to subside.

But they had to be careful not to 'find' too many balls in this way or their activities would come to the attention of the Keeper of the Green, the man in charge of all caddies. He would have started life as a caddie himself and would be fully aware of all the tricks of the trade. He had the power to strike names off the list of those registered to carry clubs and thus deprive erring caddies of their livelihood.

Old Tom Morris held this position at St Andrews for many years. The duties were wide-ranging: they included the control and upkeep of the course, making clubs and balls and carrying out repairs, giving lessons, playing with members and control of the caddies. He was effectively golf professional, green-keeper and caddie-master.

The Keeper of the Green would expect the caddies under his command to be relatively clean and moderately sober, at least during working hours. Before a round began, they would remove the member's clubs from the wooden box, rather like a small coffin, in which they were transported and stored in the clubhouse, undoing the leather strap which bound them together in a tight bundle, and carry them loose under one arm. On the first tee the golfer would pick out the most level expanse of grass and take up his stance, tapping the ground with the club-head at the precise point he wanted the caddie to make a small pyramid of wet sand on which to tee the ball. If it was the first time the caddie had carried the clubs for a particular golfer he would ask whether the player preferred a high or low tee. If he had carried for the man before he would be expected to remember.

Traditionally the sand used to make a tee was taken from the hole just completed. In fact, the very first rule of golf, committed to paper in 1744, stipulated that the ball must be teed within one club length of the hole. That conjures up a very clear idea of the condition of the greens in those early days of the game, and as play progressed the holes would become deeper and more ragged with every golfer who reached down to take a handful of sand from the bottom. Eventually the holes would become so deep that golfers or caddies had to get down on their knees, reaching at arm's length to retrieve the ball and scoop out yet more sand.

The rules were later changed so that the ball could not be teed up closer than two club lengths from the hole and finally separate teeing grounds were designated. Yet still the practice of using sand from the bottom of the hole continued. When it became more convenient for caddies to start scratching around for sand beside the new teeing grounds, club committees reacted angrily, disliking the rash of new sand-pits which were being opened up and insisting that sand was taken only from the previous hole.

A caddie dutifully tees the ball on a pyramid of sand on the spot indicated by the golfer.

127

Finally common sense prevailed and wooden or iron boxes of sand were placed at the edge of the teeing areas. This prevented the holes being enlarged and damaged during play and allowed their size to be standardized. The original tee boxes were simply receptacles for sand, but refinements followed. Those at St Andrews were raised on legs to waist height. Others were fitted with small reservoirs which kept the sand moist with a constant drip of water. In the modern game these original sand boxes are used to indicate tees and to hold litter. Many now have ball washers attached.

As well as raising the ball for tee shots, there were other uses for the abundant sand and at short holes a caddie would be expected by the more knowledgeable golfers to put a smear of wet grains on the ball to help create maximum backspin.

At the end of each round the caddie would dry off the wooden shafts and heads, treating the shafts with a thin smear of linseed oil. Iron club-heads were rubbed down with emery paper before being given a final wipe with an oily rag.

The development of the first golf bags in the 1880s should have made caddying an easier task, but like many innovations they were initially greeted with suspicion and dislike. J.H. Taylor, five times an Open Champion, credited the steward at Royal North Devon Golf Club with their invention. A former sailor skilled in sailmaking, he put together a rudimentary tube of canvas with a shoulder strap. Yet when golfers first arrived with this new piece of equipment the caddies immediately took the clubs from the bag and carried the clubs under one arm and the bag under the other. Even when the idea of the golf bag became widely accepted, the shoulder strap was ignored and until the early days of the twentieth century the whole thing was carried under the arm.

'Big' Crawford. A celebrated St Andrews caddie of the early years of the century.

By this time artificial tees made of cardboard or celluloid were being mass-produced – simple circles of material which were placed on the ground – but many golfers and caddies still stuck with the old ways and elegant little moulds were on the market so that exactly the right height and size of sand tee could be made time after time. Wooden tees did not appear until the 1930s.

Throughout the history of the game caddies have enjoyed a special relationship with golfers. Despite their often taciturn manner and unruly appearance many bag carriers of the eighteenth and nineteenth centuries were well looked after by the wealthy golfers who employed them. Many were given permanent jobs, most received gifts of clothing. Golfers would often pay for a caddie's meal. Special benefit and clothing funds were set up for them at many of the more exclusive clubs.

In St Andrews the caddies paid a deposit each year. At the end of the season deductions were made from this money to cover the upkeep of the caddie shelter, then the members of the R & A doubled the remaining total and distributed the funds among the best caddies. Boy carriers under the age of 13 were obliged to wear a cap with the R & A badge and were warned that they must continue with their education and attend Sunday school. They were forbidden to use bad language.

In 1920 a group of caddies looking for work at the Open Championship walked the 80 miles from London to Deal. Such was the sympathy for them among the professional golfers taking part

The Jigger Inn, where generations of caddies have found refreshment.

that, together with many of the wealthy club members, they started a collection to pay their train fares home. Such an act of spontaneous generosity would have been most unlikely in other than golfing circles. The caddies were suitably grateful, but it is doubtful if the money was wasted on anything so mundane as train fares when it would have provided a couple of days of excellent drinking.

It was probably because the majority of the early caddies were good golfers in their own right, far better players than the members whose clubs they carried, that they got away with expressing themselves forcibly, often caustically, and were able to form such a bond with their employers. Allied to the very dry sense of humour which is a characteristic of the east coast of Scotland, this lack of deference has produced a rich vein of stories which victims are happy to tell against themselves.

It was a member of the R & A, a wealthy landowner, who recounted how he had asked his caddie's opinion of his next opponent. 'He canna play worth a damn, sir,' was the seemingly encouraging reply. 'He's nae better than yoursel.' The golfer whose game had been assessed so brutally was not in the least offended and told the story at countless dinner parties. Equally unmoved was the member who was told by his caddie: 'You play more golf to the round than anyone I've ever seen.'

In more recent times a St Andrews caddie, who had completed a long and tiring morning round, was enjoying his normal liquid lunch in the Jigger Inn when he was persuaded, against his better judgement, to go out again in the afternoon. Almost inevitably his man found the Swilcan Burn with an approach shot to the first green. Retrieving the ball from the water, cleaning it and handing it to the golfer, the caddie advised him to pitch it well over the burn, about a yard left of the hole. After two practice swings there was a lightning fast stab at the ball and it was back in the water. The process of retrieving, cleaning and instruction was repeated, but with the same end result. On the third attempt the ball again disappeared into the burn. Dropping the bag the caddie exploded: 'I'm a caddie, not a ———- [alliterative expletive deleted] fisherman', and returned directly to the inn. For this addition to the folk-

129

lore of St Andrews he was banned from carrying for three months. Perhaps today's golfers lack the sense of humour of their forbears, but other than that the relationship between golfer and caddie at the Home of Golf remains essentially what it has been for centuries.

In a wider context, caddies are now divided into two separate groups – those who remain at championship courses like St Andrews and enjoy a light-hearted rapport with visiting golfers, and those who follow the world's tournament circuits, where the demands and the rewards are far greater. In return for a regular salary and expenses, and a healthy chunk of any prize-money, tournament caddies are expected to carry 14 clubs, two or three sweaters, a rain suit and umbrella, six gloves, a dozen balls, three hats, four bananas, six bars of chocolate, three towels and two bottles of vitamin drink. They measure every inch of the course and act, in turn, as surveyor, meteorologist, psychiatrist and confessor.

Back in 1860 caddies were the leading players and the first real professionals, but at around the turn of the last century, as the number of clubs and courses expanded at a tremendous rate, the leading caddies became full-time club professionals. From then on the two careers developed along entirely separate lines, with professionals gaining the greatest respect and authority through playing, teaching and clubmaking. The caddies' ranks continued to produce good golfers, but the best were constantly defecting to join the ranks of the professionals and those who were left were regarded more as bag carriers than experts in the game. There have always been those with no liking for regular work but with a sharp native wit and an instinct for survival; and it is they who have maintained the caddies' reputation as characters and likeable rogues.

In their way they lived up to what would appear to be the correct origins of the word 'caddie'. Although many historians cling to the explanation that it derives directly from the French word *cadet*, the name given to young men serving with the military, a much closer and more probable link has been unearthed by David Stirk in researching his excellent book *Carry Your Bag, Sir?* A dictionary of the Scottish language in 1840 cites the word 'cawdys' and quotes from descriptions of Edinburgh by a Captain Burt in 1730 in which such men are described as:

Fanny Sunesson with Nick Faldo at St Andrews for the 1990 Open, at which this celebrated partnership gained a famous victory.

Useful Blackguards, who attend coffee houses and publick places to go on errands ... wretches who lie in the streets at night ... [they are] often considerably trusted and seldom or never prove unfaithful.

The laws of libel prevent any further comment.

LEFT *Caddie 'Tip' Anderson congratulates Tony Lema on his victory at the 1964 Open. Lema later paid tribute: 'Without his help I doubt if I could have won.'* RIGHT *Gary Player and caddie pose on the Swilcan Bridge.*

Chapter 10

THE OLD COURSE

T O PLAY THE OLD COURSE at St Andrews is to plug into a direct connection with the past. Golf has been contested on this area of ancient linksland turf for some six centuries and in many ways little has changed in all that time. Yet the Old Course is not a museum piece to be fenced off and admired from a distance. The challenge it presents to modern golfers is as fresh and ever-changing as it was when our golfing ancestors struggled over the original course. Then, 11 holes were played, starting from the top of the hill behind the present R & A clubhouse and running to the shore of the River Eden estuary; there golfers turned and played the same 11 holes in reverse order. The fairways followed a narrow path between the bushes and the sand dunes and homeward players always had the right of way while those on the outward journey would have to stand aside and wait their turn. It was a confusing, frustrating and, at times, a dangerous game.

In 1764 the opening and finishing holes were taken out of play and the course reduced to 18 – a seemingly unimportant move which was eventually to set a standard adopted by the whole world. Golfers continued to play to the same holes on the outward and inward halves of the course until 1832, when double holes were cut for the first time. Not long afterwards the practice of teeing the ball on the green was abandoned and separate teeing areas were created. By this time, too, natural erosion and judicious widening had opened up larger areas of fairway.

The golfers of the early nineteenth century played the course 'backwards' – driving from the first tee to the present seventeenth green, and then following the inland holes to the turn, with the seaward holes forming the second nine. But the attractions of playing the course in the modern order became apparent to many local golfers and for a period of some 30 to 40 years the layout of the course was changed from day to day or week to week, the two alternatives being known as the left-hand and right-hand courses.

It was not until 1870 that a separate first green was constructed just beyond the twists and turns of the Swilcan Burn. It was probably at that time that the permanent switch to the use of the right-hand course for all major events took place, although the other course was

Looking over the Old Course with the second green in the foreground and the New and Jubilee Courses in the distance.

133

still regularly played. Records for the two courses continued into the last decade of the century, but it was certainly not intended that the Amateur Championship of 1886, the first to be played at St Andrews, should be contested on the left-hand course. However, Old Tom Morris, who was by then 65 years old, was still Keeper of the Green and it was his responsibility to set up the course for the Championship. By a considerable oversight he failed to ensure the modern course was in play on the first morning and Horace Hutchinson won the title on the wrong course.

The change was not popular with everyone and James Balfour complained that the fifth hole was

> altered more than any other on the links. The tee stroke used always to be played to the right of the big bunker with the uncouth name unless some huge driver swiped over H— at one immortal blow.

He went on to describe how the hole was then played through the Elysian Fields and over the Beardies to the green. This is a perfect description of playing the fourteenth hole backwards to the thirteenth green and the name of the 'uncouth bunker' which Balfour could not bring himself to mention was, of course, Hell.

Since the permanent switch from left- to right-hand course, very little has changed on the Old Course. In the early 1900s additional bunkers were put in to the right of the second, third, fourth and fifth fairways to replace the outcrops of whin bushes which once filled the open spaces. And a bunker in the midst of the vast expanse of first and eighteenth fairways was filled in just before the First World War. The course is now watered with an automatic system and it is much easier to stop the modern golf ball on greens far softer than those our golfing forefathers would have recognized, but in essence the problems faced by golfers in the dying years of the twentieth century are those which existed when the game was born.

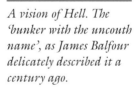

A vision of Hell. The 'bunker with the uncouth name', as James Balfour delicately described it a century ago.

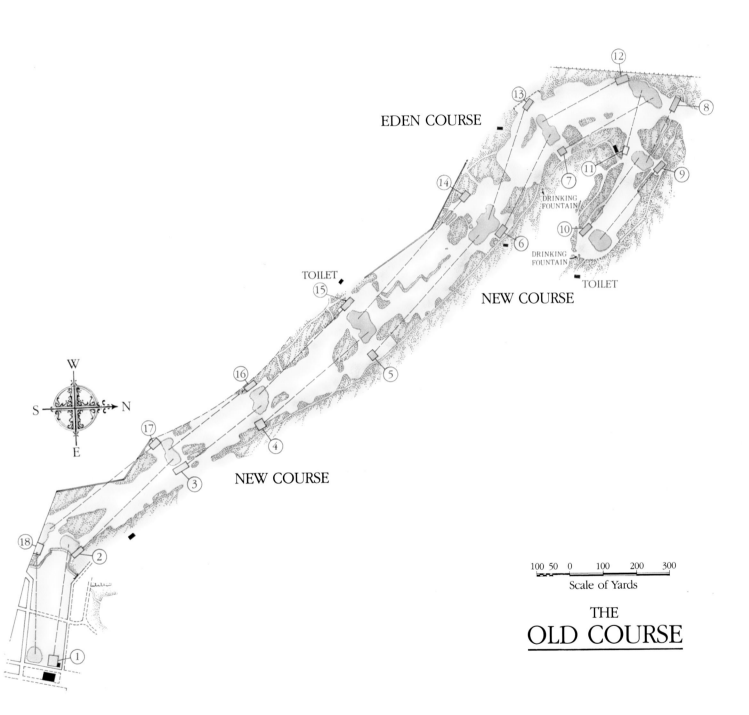

EDEN COURSE

NEW COURSE

DRINKING
FOUNTAIN

DRINKING
FOUNTAIN

TOILET

TOILET

NEW COURSE

W
S — N
E

100 50 0   100   200   300
Scale of Yards

THE
OLD COURSE

Two challenges face the player on the first tee: the critical eyes of the spectators on the terrace of the Royal & Ancient clubhouse behind (RIGHT) and the thin line which marks the course of the Swilcan Burn in front of the green (BELOW).

Hole 1

Par 4. 370 yards. Burn

The opening hole of the Old Course presents a double challenge. One is clearly visible, a snaking ribbon of water that slices across the front of the green. The other is invisible, intangible.

Even hardened tournament professionals admit to being affected by the aura of tradition and history which hangs heavily in the air. Under the intimidating gaze of the large R & A clubhouse windows and the ever-curious parade of golfing pilgrims, the tee shot on the first hole of the Old Course can bring a twitch to the strongest nerves. As each new supplicant at the golfing shrine steps forward the general hub-bub in this most public of places reduces to a whisper. Only the circling seagulls ignore the etiquette of the ancient game, screeching in seeming derision.

Other than that unavoidable tension at the tee, the first shot is simple. The target of the combined first and eighteenth fairways is more than a hundred yards wide, although the prevailing south-west wind, against and from the left, can convert a gentle fade into a damned slice as it edges the ball ever closer to the white fence and the out of bounds area towards the beach.

The second shot can be anything from a floated sand-wedge to a full-blooded three-wood depending on the season and the weather, but most often falls in the mid- to short-iron range. The Swilcan Burn, one of the skinniest water hazards in golf, collects an incredible number of golf balls despite its lack of size, even the mighty Jack Nicklaus falling prey to its hypnotic menace.

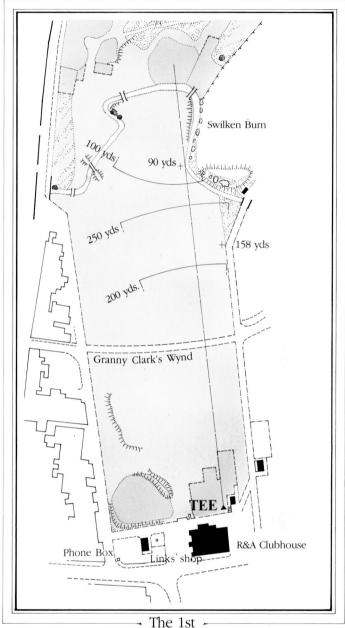

The 1st
THE BURN 370 yds.

Because the fairway and green are set at exactly the same level, separated only by the narrow strip of water, the second shot can be difficult to judge. Better to take an extra club and finish at the back of the green, although as American professional Tom Shaw discovered in the 1970 Open Championship, even ultra-safe play can have its problems. With the pin set close to the water, his long putt from the back of the green trickled over the edge into the burn. Returning to the fairway side of the hazard, he took a penalty drop and promptly chipped into the hole for an unlikely opening five.

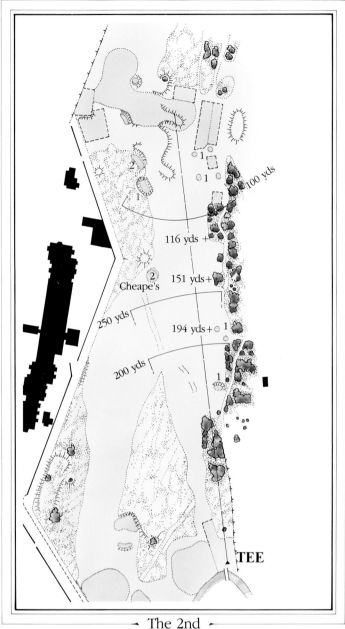

100 yds

116 yds +

151 yds+

Cheape's

2

250 yds

194 yds+

200 yds

TEE

→ The 2nd ←
THE DYKE 411 yds.

Hole 2.

Par 4. 411 yards. Dyke

The problems posed by the Old Course are much easier to handle with modern equipment than they were in the early years of the game's development. Strong shafts allow iron shots to be hit with a firm downward blow which generates maximum backspin and a high trajectory, while new golf-ball technology gives players the chance to screw the ball to a stop on the hardest putting surfaces. The second hole is a classic example of how evolving equipment has taken many of the terrors out of the original challenge; yet it remains one of the most respected two-shotters in the game, claiming more shots than it surrendered in recent championships.

In the days of hickory shafts the narrow gap between Cheape's bunker on the left and the mass of whin bushes on the right was the only viable line for the tee shot. For it was only from the right side of the fairway that a clear line to the pin could be gained, essential when the second shot had to be hit on a low, running trajectory with a brassie or spoon. Any tee shot to the left puts a ridge of humps and hollows and two bunkers on the line to the championship pin position. This would have been a virtually impossible shot a hundred years ago.

Today's big-hitting tournament specialists, in contrast, can cover the same ground with a booming drive to any part of the fairway and a high-flying nine-iron. Only when the wind turns against them and the second shot has to be played with a long-iron do they become aware of the mean test this hole can present and learn to respect the skill of those who mastered its challenge in earlier days.

The Old Course can be played relatively safely by aiming left off almost every tee. The greens are so large that even modestly handicapped players can reach most with comparative ease. But to get the ball close to the championship pin positions, today's title-chasers have to follow closely in the footsteps of history's heroes – players like Old Tom Morris and Bobby Jones.

Looking back from the seventeenth fairway to the town and the Royal & Ancient clubhouse.

139

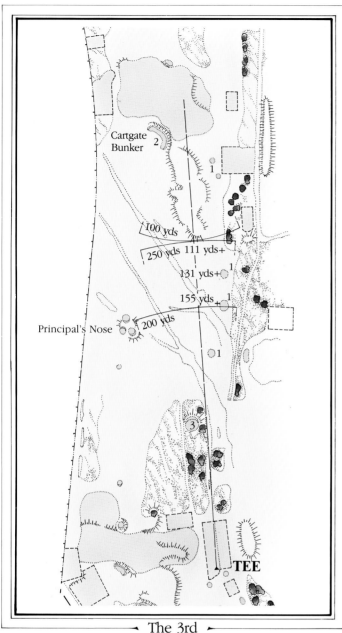

The 3rd
CARTGATE OUT 352 yds.

Hole 3

Par 4. 352 (371)* yards. Cartgate Out

The chance of an early birdie presents itself here, but once again the right side of the fairway offers the best chance to attack the pin. A row of three bunkers and a few scattered bushes threaten this line from the tee, but the main test comes in flighting the ball into the green.

The putting surface is set at a slightly higher level then the fairway, with a ridge jutting out of the left side and running back towards the player. This ridge drops into a hollow occupied by two small bunkers to the right and falls sharply from the left edge of the green into Cartgate bunker. Any tee shot held too far left leaves an approach which must carry this bunker into a green which slopes away towards the back and right at this point. Any ball moving right will run off the green down towards the next tee and an over-hit second shot can find the sunken portion of the green at back right.

Keeping the tee shot close to the right edge of the fairway sets up a good angle to pitch the ball on to the ridge and run it into the left side of the green, or to carry it all the way for hole positions further back and right.

Bing Crosby scored an early success here when he played the British Amateur Championship in 1950. Drawn against local character J.K. Wilson, Crosby proved his golfing pedigree with birdies at the first and third holes, but went on to lose the match. He later donated a trophy which is played for annually on the Old Course by senior golfers.

* Yardage distances in brackets refer to Championship tees.

Hole 4

Par 4. 419 (463) yards. Ginger Beer

When Bobby Jones attempted to win the 1930 Amateur on his way to capturing the grand slam of Open and Amateur events in Britain and America in the same season, he might have acknowledged a nod from the gods as he played the fourth hole in his opening match. Drawn against Sid Roper, an ex-coalminer who played the first five holes in strict par, Jones was five under par for the same stretch and four up. He hit a tremendous drive at the fourth, but drew the ball 300 yards into Cottage bunker, a long stretch of sand that separates the fourth and fifteenth fairways. The bunker is narrow and quite deep, but Jones managed to get the ball up quickly and still make the carry to the edge of the green, where the ball kept running until it vanished in the hole for an eagle two.

The hole is longer now, but big-hitters can still reach that same bunker if they choose to hit the ball slightly left off the tee and over a rising plateau. The narrow ribbon of fairway is clearly defined to the right of this raised ground, but with stunted fingers of sloping rough jutting out from the plateau and bunkers squeezing in on the other side, there are barely twenty paces of cut grass to aim at.

The shot into the green is obstructed by a large, rounded mound which extends right up to the putting surface and throws off any ball running towards the left half of the green. A short-iron second shot can clear it with ease and be confidently hit at the pin, but into a north-westerly breeze it plays an important part when conditions call for a long, raking second shot.

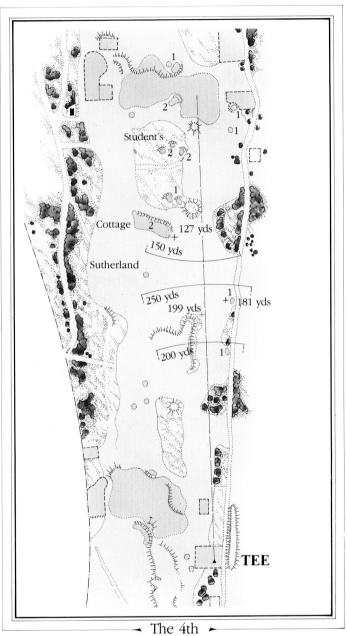

The 4th
GINGER BEER 419 yds.

The large green is deep enough to hold a long-iron approach and climbs steeply towards the back, dropping away sharply into sand at the left and rolling gently down to the right.

Like the second, this is a fine links hole which gives very little away. During the 1984 Open it conceded only 29 birdies.

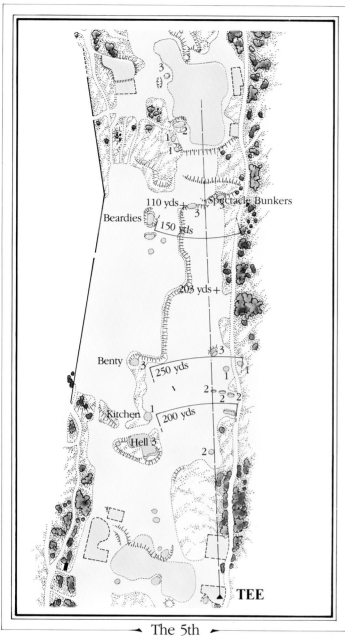

The 5th
HOLE O' CROSS OUT 514 yds.

Hole 5

Par 5. 514 (564) yards. Hole O'Cross Out

In contrast to the previous hole, the long fifth, the first of only two par fives on the course, is an absolute push-over for the pros. It is consistently the easiest hole when championships are played at St Andrews and birdies are as common as pars.

Length alone has ceased to be a problem for the players who win major events. Even when new courses stretch holes to well over 600 yards, players like Sandy Lyle and John Daly still manage to cover the distance in two enormous blows. On old-established links courses, the option of extending holes often does not exist; nor is it desirable. Certainly the Old Course should not be tampered with.

The main difficulty at the fifth is in judging the line of the tee shot to avoid the nest of seven bunkers that lurks on the right side of the fairway between 240 and 300 yards out. The banks of several of these traps are clearly visible from the tee, but many first-time players fail to appreciate just how wide a berth they should be given. Jack Nicklaus was caught three times in four rounds when he first played the Open Championship at St Andrews in 1964. Each time he aimed a little further left – and still finished in the sand. When he returned to win the title after a play-off with Doug Sanders six years later he had learned his lesson well, avoiding the bunkers in all five rounds.

Tony Lema had never seen the Old Course when he arrived for the 1964 Open, but quickly learned to take the advice of local caddie Tip Anderson, the man who made a career out of carrying for Arnold Palmer. 'I always felt I could hit much closer to the traps than Tip recommended. Yet I saw many players hit drives I thought were perfect, but they kept finishing in the sand', said Lema, who gave much of the credit for his run-away victory to Anderson.

What is not evident from the tee is that a section of fairway left of the bunkers is full of swales and hollows that actually channel the ball towards the sand. And the prevailing wind from the left just makes it that much easier for tee shots to run out of fairway. Yet, unless the ball finishes tight under the lip, most often players can still escape with par. Even flip-

The fifth and thirteenth share what is, perhaps, the largest green in the world. The flag for the fifth hole is to the right and that for the thirteenth to the left in the background.

ping the ball out sideways makes it possible to hit the target in three, although a ridge, bitten into by deep bunkers on either side, with a deep hollow beyond, lies across the face of the green.

But hitting the green in regulation does not guarantee getting down in par. Possibly the largest putting surface in the world, the combined fifth and thirteenth measures some 90 yards by 70. The twelfth green at Augusta National, home of the US Masters, would fit into its one-acre extent 21 times.

143

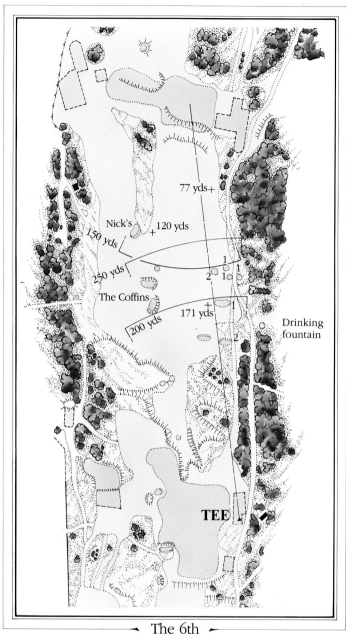

The 6th
HEATHERY OUT 374 yds.

Hole 6

Par 4. 374 (416) yards. Heathery Out

There is an element of uncertainty about both shots at the sixth. This is the only truly blind drive on the course, with a carry of close to 200 yards over heather- and gorse-covered hillocks from the championship tee down to the hidden fairway.

A line of three bunkers rejoicing in the name of Coffins separates this fairway from the thirteenth on the left, and another deep sandpit, further on the same line and called Nick's, is presumably named after the devil himself rather than any contemporary tournament professional. There is ample fairway between these ominous-sounding bunkers and those on the right, which are themselves flanked by whin bushes, but there is far more to the approach shot than the simple pitch it appears to require.

Towards the green the ground rises slightly, with the crest of a low ridge making it impossible to see the bottom of the pin, unless the hole cut is in the extreme right side. Also totally hidden from the golfer's view is the deep depression between the ridge and the green.

Many a seemingly perfect high-flying pitch shot to a forward pin position on this green just catches the top of the rise and falls back into the hollow. That sets up a difficult putt which must climb the steep slope then fall away softly down the contours on the other side.

A typical links golf shot, perfected several centuries ago, is often the more telling option for the approach than trying to carry the ball into the green. Keeping the hands well ahead of the ball and minimizing leg and body action, the low pitch-and-run is played almost exclusively with the arms, bumping the ball over the fairway ridge and letting it run through the hollow to the pin. It is a shot which has paid handsome dividends for generations of links players and is particularly effective against or across a strong wind.

Hole 7

Par 4. 359 (372) yards. High Out

This is traditionally known as the start of the famous Old Course loop – a run of four short par fours and two par threes which double back on themselves so that the eleventh hole crosses the seventh. It is the chance to set up a good score, a form of insurance before facing the exacting test of the final six homeward holes.

Curtis Strange was certainly aware of the vulnerability of the loop when he faced Greg Norman in the play-off for third and fourth place in the Dunhill team event in 1987. His fine tee shot carried the ridge of high ground which marks the driving limit for most handicap golfers and he was left with nothing more than a wedge over the depths of Shell bunker to the raised, sloping green. On a totally windless day, with the greens receptive in the damp atmosphere, he stopped the ball close to the pin and holed for the first of what proved to be a run of six consecutive birdies. Norman's two-under-par 70 was beaten by eight shots as Strange set a new course record of 62.

Those who do not hit the ball as far as the tournament professionals have a narrow fairway gap of no more than a dozen yards to the right of the ridge which erupts in the middle of the fairway. A drive to the left of this raised ground flirts with Admiral's bunker, but offers the chance of a longer approach between, rather than over, two more expanses of sand. Shell bunker, which runs across the face of the raised green, is second in size only to Hell at the fourteenth.

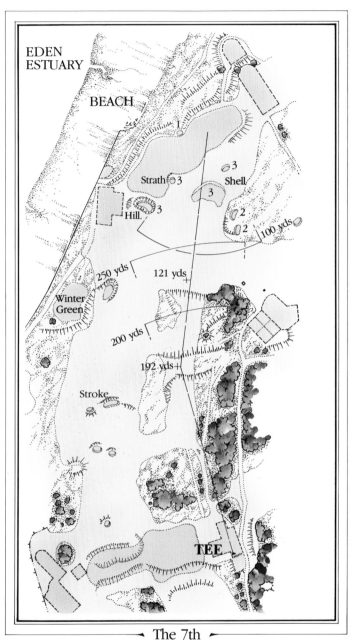

The 7th
HIGH HOLE OUT 359 yds.

The faces of many Old Course bunkers are so steep that they have to be regularly rebuilt with walls of turf. It takes more than five acres of cut turf to complete the job.

LEFT *The seventh green, clearly showing the dangerous Shell bunker to the right and, on the left, Strath bunker, which threatens players on the eleventh hole which shares the green (see page 151).*

145

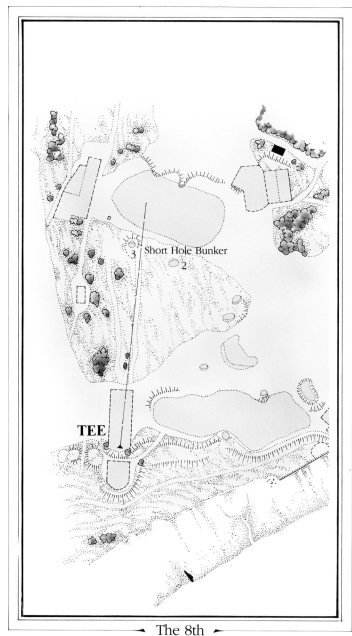

The 8th
SHORT HOLE 166 yds.

RIGHT *Players approaching the eighth green, Short Hole bunker is to their left.*

Hole 8

Par 3. 166 (178) yards. Short

Those responsible for naming the holes and the bunkers on the Old Course did not have to draw too deeply on the well of inspiration when they considered the first of only two par-three holes and its main feature, Short Hole bunker.

A new, raised tee which extends the hole to almost 200 yards is often called into play for everyday use, but is not employed during the Open. From the championship tee the hole is completely flat. A shallow bank, starting beyond the left edge of the green, increases in height as it edges across the front of the putting surface, culminating in the open mouth of Short Hole bunker.

Typically, the hole is cut behind the bunker, the rear bank of which slopes down into the green, making it difficult to drop the ball just beyond its grasp and hold position. The bunker itself is small in diameter, but has a deep, vertical face. Trying to finesse the ball close to the hole from here is an exercise in futility, making sure of the recovery is the prime concern.

With the prevailing wind behind and from the right the majority of shots finish well towards the back of this deep green, which measures 45 yards from front to back. It is one of the more subtly contoured putting surfaces on the course and its vast size – it sweeps away more than 80 yards to the right to form the tenth green – tends to create an optical illusion of complete flatness which is very deceptive. For there is, in fact, a shallow spine which runs diagonally through the green, causing putts to swing unexpectedly off line.

Hole 9

Par 4. 307 (356) yards. End

Ginger Beer, the curious name given to the fourth hole, would have been more aptly applied to the ninth and would certainly have been an improvement on the prosaic title it now bears. Old Da', or Daw, Anderson, whose son Jamie won the Open three times in succession from 1877, dispensed non-alcoholic ginger beer from his stall at this point throughout the summer months, retreating to the fourth in winter when many golfers would play only four or five holes out before heading back towards the town. They were known, on those cold days, to enliven his refreshment with a decent measure of brandy.

In its original form this was a hole with no fairway, just one vast expanse of heather from tee to green. It was not until the mid 1800s that Old Tom Morris decided to turf the last 150 yards into the green. Two bunkers, 70 and 50 yards short of the green, are clearly visible, unlike the majority at St Andrews; but there is also another small sand trap just off the left edge of the green, hidden by the banks of whins which crowd in towards the putting surface at this point. Heather still frames the left side of the generous fairway.

Compared with most of the earlier holes and those yet to come, the ninth is a picture of innocence, seemingly susceptible to a birdie blitz by long-driving professionals who can often reach the green downwind. Yet it provides a classic links test, for there is no definition around the green to aid judgement of distance for those who do not reach it from the tee. The fairway runs directly into the large circular green and the flat ground continues behind the putting surface, giving no backdrop against which to judge an approach shot. Thus, while it is true that not many of the leading players find any trouble at this hole, far fewer birdies are recorded here than its innocuous appearance would suggest.

There have, however, been a few spectacular eagles such as that which helped Jock Hutchison win the 1921 Championship (see Chapter 5) and that scored by Tony Jacklin during his ill-fated attempt in the 1970 event, described in Chapter 6.

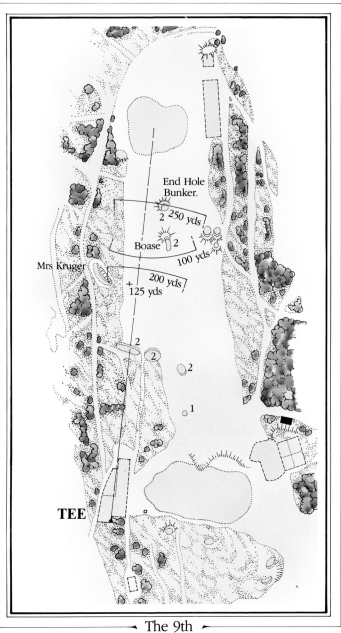

The 9th
END HOLE 307 yds.

OVERLEAF
Approaching the ninth hole with Boase and End Hole bunkers directly ahead.

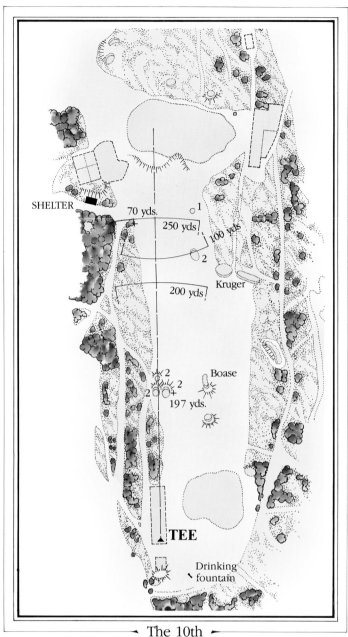

SHELTER

70 yds.

250 yds

100 yds

2

Kruger

200 yds

2
2
2
4

Boase

197 yds.

TEE

Drinking
fountain

The 10th
BOBBY JONES 318 yds.

Hole 10

Par 4. 318 (342) yards. Bobby Jones

The naming of this hole after the greatest amateur golfer of all time does not commemorate any astonishing feat accomplished over its modest length, but is a permanent monument to the respect in which he was held by the golfing community of St Andrews. The decision to name a hole on the Old Course after the man who won the Amateur and Open Championships of Britain and America in the same season of 1930, was taken in 1972, the year after his death. The choice of which hole was to carry his name was simple. The tenth was the only one on the course not already named by history or happenstance.

Jones felt that his deep knowledge of the course allowed him to play it with patience and restraint, while his opponents might encounter problems as a result of their lack of respect for its ever-changing challenge. From that point of view it is appropriate that this hole bears his name. Like the ninth, to which it runs parallel, but in the opposite direction, it can be driven, yet it is never a hole to treat with contempt. Most often the prevailing wind will leave a short-iron approach over rising ground to a green which slopes away to the back.

Getting there in two is never a problem. Getting the ball close enough for the obvious birdie chance is another matter. At about 250 yards the target area narrows between a deep bunker on the right and bushes on the left. In order to get better control of the approach shot many pros will lay up from the tee to leave a full wedge or nine-iron with which they hope to work the ball close to the hole. Britain's Ryder Cup captain Bernard Gallacher, not one of the game's renowned long-hitters, once hammered his tee shot to this green, but forgot Bobby Jones' advice. In a bold effort to capture an eagle he four-putted.

Hole 11

Par 3. 172 yards. High Hole In

St Andrews officials missed a golden opportunity when it was decided to name a hole on the Old Course after Bobby Jones. Instead of taking the easy option of choosing the tenth as described above, they could have taken the bold step of re-naming High Hole In for the man who dominated the game so completely. For the eleventh was a hole which had a great effect on Jones' career and which he later copied, as the fourth at Augusta National, home of the US Masters, and which, as described in Chapter 5, was the scene of his abrupt withdrawal from the 1921 Open.

The hole which triggered Jones' outburst of temperament continues to have the same effect on golfers of all calibres to this day. The raised green is set against the estuary of the River Eden and slopes fiercely towards the front. On days of high wind the exposed surface is very reluctant to hold the ball.

To get to the green the ball has to be threaded through a gap which can seem fairly generous on a still summer day, and frighteningly narrow against a gusting wind. The small Strath bunker on the right, behind which the pin is often set, gathers balls into its depths from a much wider catchment area. On the left the ground falls vertically into Hill bunker, from which a recovery must clear a face some 12 feet high.

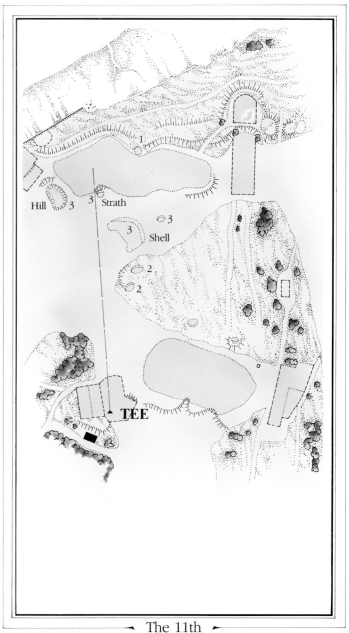

The 11th
HIGH HOLE IN 172 yds.

Any tee shot moving to the right is likely to continue its downward and wayward journey until it finishes up closer to the hole on the seventh, which shares this elongated ribbon of green, leaving a return putt of anything up to 60 yards.

LEFT *The formidable face of Hill bunker at the eleventh hole.*

151

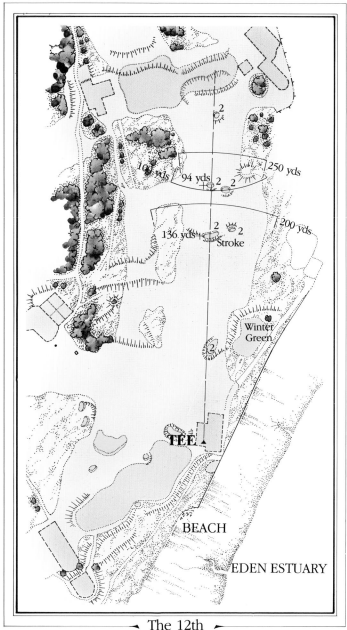

The 12th
HEATHERY IN 316 yds.

Hole 12
Par 4. 316 yards. Heathery In

From a tee perched close above the waters of the wide River Eden estuary a slightly rumpled but seemingly hazard-free fairway falls gently away towards one mounded bunker just short of the green.

Sounds simple, but in reality nothing could be further from the case. Those who lack the ability to carry the ball 225 yards into the narrowest part of the target area should ignore the centre of the fairway completely. For just beyond a slight ridge, and within driving distance of virtually every golfer playing the Old Course, a long thin bunker, closely resembling a tank trap, runs across the line of play. To the right of its outflung arm a sand-filled pit like a small bomb crater catches many a ball that thinks it has escaped to safety. The next ridge, some forty yards further on, conceals another pair of bunkers from whose depths it is almost impossible to reach the green.

The average golfer should therefore avoid the centre of the fairway like the plague, while the pros will normally fly all the trouble and can often drive the green. That is what Tom Watson was attempting in the final round of the 1984 Open. But he hooked his tee shot into thick bushes which cover the slopes to the left of the green. After a penalty drop he pitched and two-putted for a five, where he might confidently have expected a birdie to finish off the six holes of the loop. This was probably a more costly error than the much talked about shot he dropped at the seventeenth on the way to the runner-up spot behind Seve Ballesteros.

The green itself is wide but shallow, with the raised rear section no more than 12 paces deep. Driving close to the green offers the opportunity to run the ball up the slope with more control. From further out it presents a very small target. The run of holes from here to the final green is on the oldest, longest used – and most abused – part of the Old Course. This was the stretch of land in play when the outward and inward holes were o the same narrow fairways and to the same hole positions. As separate holes and double greens were introduced in about 1830 the fairways and greens were extended towards the North Sea. Yet in those days the course was played in a clockwise direction – not the anti-clockwise loop that it describes today. Thus it is only when looking back up the expanse of the twelfth fairway to the eleventh green that one obtains a perspective of the hole as it was originally played, with at least a glimpse of the trouble that lies in the centre of the fairway.

Hole 13

Par 4. 398 (425) yards. Hole O'Cross In

This is the point where experienced Old Course players start to protect the score they already have in the
bank. Unless the situation is desperate this homeward
stretch of holes is no place to force the pace.

The ideal position for the tee shot at this classic
links hole is directly beyond the last of the three
Coffin bunkers which mark the only physical boundary between its fairway and that of the adjoining sixth.
But beware, many hopes of a good score have been
buried right here.

Angling the tee shot left to borrow the sixth fairway can give a clear line to the green, but anything
drifting too far will be blocked out by gorse
enshrouded hummocks. Keeping safely to the right of
the Coffin bunkers will leave a second shot from
below a steep bank.

A narrow tongue of green sticks out at the player,
but falls away left and right and to reach the main part
of the putting surface the ball must carry bunkers,
rough swales, mounds and whins. It can be as little as
a wedge, but there are days when even the strongest
hitters are forced to hit a full four- or five-iron. With
the pin set close behind the bunker on the right, or
just beyond the rough hollow on the left, it is a hole
which exacts a harsh penalty on those who get it
wrong.

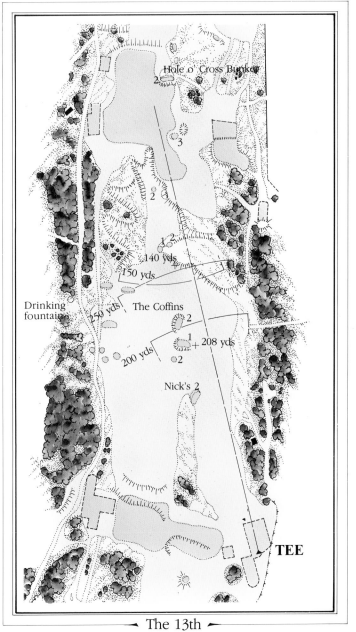

The 13th
HOLE O' CROSS IN 398 yds.

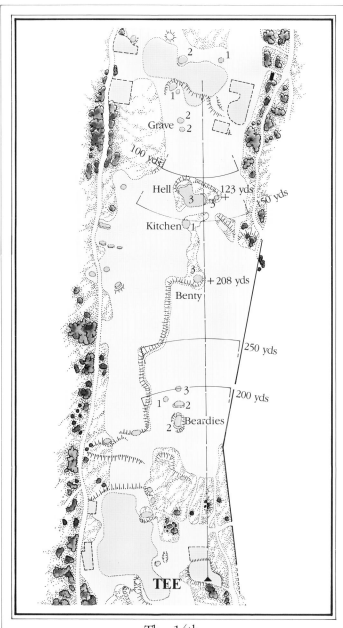

The 14th
LONG HOLE 523 yds

Hole 14

Par 5. 523 (567) yards. Long

Modern par-five holes, no matter how much they are lengthened and tricked up, are treated with virtual contempt by today's professionals. If they do not make four they feel they have dropped a shot. Not so on the fourteenth hole of the Old Course, where average scores in the Open Championship have often been well over par. On many occasions it has proved to be the second most difficult hole on the course, runner-up only to the notorious seventeenth.

From the championship tee the out-of-bounds stone wall which separates the Old Course from the Eden marches arrow-straight for some 200 yards before veering off to the right to accommodate a more generous width of fairway. Yet the line of aim has to be inside the wall, which leaves only a narrow gap before it encounters the group of four bunkers on the left known as the Beardies. A carry of 250 yards is necessary if the ball is to be driven safely beyond the sand.

If this is achieved the player enters a blissful zone of wide, flat fairway called the Elysian Fields, but any feeling of tranquillity they might inspire will be short-lived, for a battle with Hell lies ahead. This is the massive expanse of sand, some 28 yards from front to back, which lies below the end of the elevated fairway. From the back of the Beardies to the far side of Hell is a carry of well over 200 yards. There is very little room to the right, much more to the left, on the fifth fairway; this is also the preferred route for it offers an easier approach to the green which is severely banked at the front, mostly so at the right, with the putting surface dropping away from the player towards the back. The main danger of taking the left hand route to by-pass Hell is that the third shot into the slope at the front of the green could catch one of the two bunkers called Grave. They are certainly well-named, not as deep as a decent burial plot, but hardly larger.

When he first played the Open at St Andrews in 1964, Jack Nicklaus managed to avoid the devilish and funereal problems by hitting a deliberate hook from the tee on to the fifth fairway, then smacked the ball straight on to the green with as little as a five-iron and never more than a three. There are not many in the modern game who can beat that.

Hole 15

Par 4. 401 (413) yards. Cartgate In

Sutherland bunker, a tiny, circular pit some two hundred yards from the tee, is a continuing monument to people power. Those unlucky enough to get caught in its grasp in the middle of a vast expanse of untroubled fairway can console themselves that it is part of the folklore of St Andrews. Named for a member of the R & A who, it was claimed, spent more time in it than he did at home, it was filled in by order of the Greens Committee in 1885.

But then, as now, the golfers of St Andrews objected to the traditions and history of their course being abused. Under cover of darkness a group of local stalwarts took the sort of decisive action that is unfortunately missing today. Armed with spades, they restored the bunker to its former glory and it continues to plague golfers to this day.

As with so many of the St Andrews greens, this one falls away from the player, a legacy of the time when the course was played in the opposite direction. The mound on the left of the green contains a bunker, the one on the right will merely throw the ball off into a grassy hollow.

After the multitude of problems at the long fourteenth, this hole offers a slight respite before the final assault, but it is still a challenge which will only give up a stroke if played perfectly.

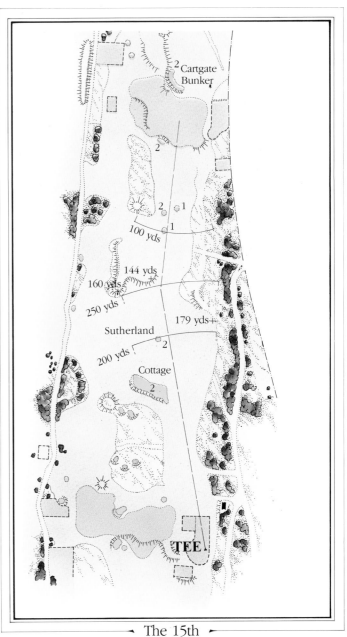

The 15th
CARTGATE IN 401 yds.

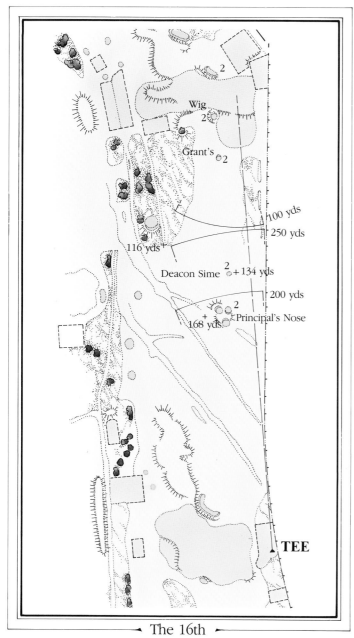

The 16th
CORNER OF THE DYKE 351 yds.

RIGHT Looking back down the sixteenth fairway, with the disused railway line clearly visible to the left.

Even when the railway was in existence it was not always out of bounds. Many a golfer has climbed over the fence to attempt a recovery shot from between the railway sleepers and, hopefully, between trains.

Hole 16

Par 4. 351 (382) yards. Corner of the Dyke

There are four ways to play the sixteenth. The virtually unanimous opinion of today's globe-trotting tournament professionals is that the sensible option is to stay well left of the central bunker known as the Principal's Nose. For them the straight line route between the bunker and the out-of-bounds fence on the right is strictly for amateurs.

It was Bobby Locke who introduced a third route. He would knock the ball far out to the right, over what used to be the railway line, and hook it back with his familiar, lazy action.

Arnold Palmer, not surprisingly, took an altogether more direct approach – but only in practice. Before the 1960 Open Championship he astounded his caddie and everyone else by smashing the ball on to the green and holing from 4 feet for an incredible eagle two. Yet he was never tempted to try it once the Open was underway. The penalty for failure was too great.

The Principal's Nose has two completely hidden nostrils immediately behind the prominent mound that can be seen from the tee. Thirty yards further on, Deacon Sime waits for the imprudent golfer who takes the direct line to the pin in the belief that the undulating fairway contains no hidden problems.

From the pro position on the left, the second shot is usually no more than a medium or short iron, threatened by Wig bunker in the corner of the L-shaped two-tier green.

Hole 17

Par 4. 461 yards. Road

An entire book could be devoted to the golfing dramas which have unfolded over the tortuous yardage of this infamous hole. In essence its challenge is uncomplicated. The hole dog-legs to the right and the ideal position from which to attack the green is from the extreme right edge of the fairway.

Thus the bolder the line a player takes over the out-of-bounds area which creates the dog-leg, the greater the tactical reward. The long, narrow, raised green runs away at an angle from front right to back left, with the road from which the hole gets its name close behind its entire length. The contours which run up to the top level of the green fall sharply into a deep pot bunker which has been clawed out of the front left side.

The hole took on added terrors with the coming of the railway and the improvement in golf equipment. It was originally played as a par five, and there were not many players who could attempt a long carry over the wall with hickory shafts and gutta balls. The majority were content to keep the drive out to the left, place the ball well to the right with the second shot and then face a long approach from the correct side of the fairway.

By the time that players were regularly cutting the corner with their improved rubber-wound golf balls, and later with steel shafts, the area beyond the wall had become a railway goods yard and large storage sheds blocked out the view. Anyone cutting the corner now had to hit over the sheds to a hidden fairway. Then, for a period of some twenty years, the famous sheds disappeared. In a masterpiece of forward planning a modern, railway-owned hotel was built on the site of the old goods yard. There was to be a return to the luxurious days of the past when passengers could step straight from the train into the hotel. Unfortunately, by the time the building was completed the railway line had been closed. In the space of less than two years St Andrews had gained an ugly hotel and lost its link to the national rail network.

Before the old railway sheds were demolished it was agreed that the hotel would replace them with a metal and mesh framework showing the outline of their former shape so that the playing characteristics of the hole would remain unchanged. But the fact that golfers could, as it were, see straight through the sheds somehow took away an essential element

→ The 17th ←
THE ROAD HOLE 461 yds.

157

from the hole, and when the Old Course Hotel was later transferred to private ownership and extended the sheds were faithfully reproduced. All that's missing now is the sound of the steam trains rattling and whistling past and the lumps of coal that would often be thrown at those bold enough to climb the wall in search of a wayward ball.

The white painted Jigger Inn, now embraced by the hotel extension, was once the station master's house. It still overlooks a hole which has baffled high-handicap amateurs and skilled tournament players in almost equal numbers.

Amateurs in any doubt about the tee shot should aim at the spire of Hope Park Church on the town skyline. Those who can confidently hit the ball straight and carry it some 250 yards through the air can aim at the last letter of the sign painted on the sheds – but any hint of a fade could end up in Room 216.

Hole 18

Par 4. 354 yards. Tom Morris

And so we are back where we started – a simple par-four hole with the widest fairway in golf and only the intimidatory factor of the shops, hotels, houses and golf clubs running the length of the out-of-bounds fence on the right to worry about. And the people, of course.

No matter the season of the year or the time of day, there are always people around the final hole of the Old Course. In summer there could be hundreds. It is probably the largest gallery most amateurs will play to in a lifetime of golf.

Aim the tee shot at the R & A clubhouse clock and no matter the degree of deviation it should still finish comfortably in play, although there are those who have missed this vast expanse by ridiculous margins. It is the second shot that causes the problems – even for the pros who can knock it within spitting distance of the green.

The whole putting surface falls sharply from right to left and, apart from the right third of its 50-yard width, it is fronted by a deep depression which has become known as the Valley of Sin. Certainly the sins of under-hitting approach shots and of blasphemy are regularly seen and heard by those leaning on the nearby railings.

Back in 1933 another American, Leo Diegel, suffered an even worse fate on this green. With a short putt to win the Open title he missed the ball completely. Veteran golf columnist Bernard Darwin wrote simply: 'He missed the first putt by the greatest possible margin.' If he had holed his next attempt it would have put him in a play-off, but he yipped it a foot wide of the hole.

It is only in modern times that the areas outside the course have been designated out of bounds. There was not even a fence down the side of the final fairway until the 1950s. There is a well authenticated case of a local golfer who took advantage of the extra space this allowed. His wild tee shot passed behind the buildings which face out on to the Old Course. Pursuing his ball through the traffic on the main road into St Andrews he found himself opposite Granny Clark's Wynd, the roadway that crosses the first and eighteenth fairways. He had a clear view back to the course, putted between the houses, pitched on to the green and holed the putt for as unlikely a four as will ever be scored.

When local veterans leaning on the fence behind the last green say that they have seen everything there is to see in golf they do not exaggerate.

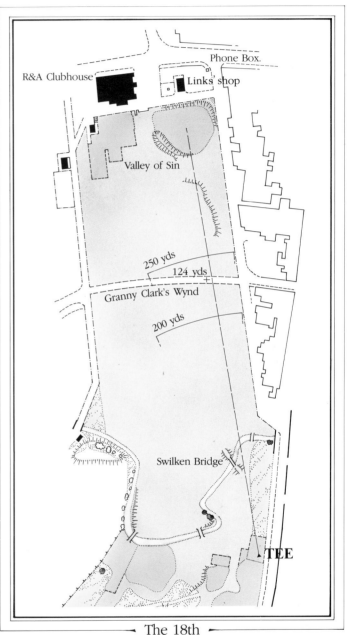

The 18th
TOM MORRIS 354 yds.

OVERLEAF: *The approach to the eighteenth green with the Valley of Sin in the foreground.*
INSET *Looking back over the Swilcan Bridge to the eighteenth tee and the green of the seventeenth.*

Chapter 11

THE OTHER COURSES

F OR NEWCOMERS, it is difficult to adjust to St Andrews' timescales. It may not, for example, seem very significant that the New Course celebrates its centenary in 1995 – for, by comparison with its next-door neighbour, where the game has been played for close on 600 years, it is still very much in the first flush of youth. Yet stop, for a moment, and consider that a century ago golf courses were still comparatively rare, and that the first American course was barely seven years old. In St Andrews, 'New' is very much a comparative term.

The New Course

St Andrews' second course was proposed by the Town Council and the Royal and Ancient Golf Club in 1883, when both bodies were concerned over the number of golfers trying to play the Old Course. The process by which the linksland to the north and west of the city passed into possession of the Town Council at this time has already been described. The Links Act of 1894 which gave the Council the right to buy the linksland also made the R & A responsible for the design and construction of the New Course, which they leased from the Council for a payment of £125 a year for 60 years.

There was no shortage of land on which to construct the New Course. Vast areas of linksland had been left between the Old Course and the coast as the sea continued to recede. In fact the New follows closely on the model set by the Old Course, and snuggles tightly up against it over much of the outward nine holes. Many a pulled tee shot on the first hole of the New makes an unintended appearance near the second green of the Old, the compliment being immediately returned when sliced drives from the Old's third hole pepper the vicinity of the first green of its younger neighbour. The junior partner follows the Old Course out to the Eden estuary, then loops back on itself in imitation of the Old, before following a straight course back to the ancient city. There are no artificial boundaries between the two courses – sand dunes and whin bushes forming their own natural barriers – and there are no out-of-bounds penalties for straying from one to the other.

163

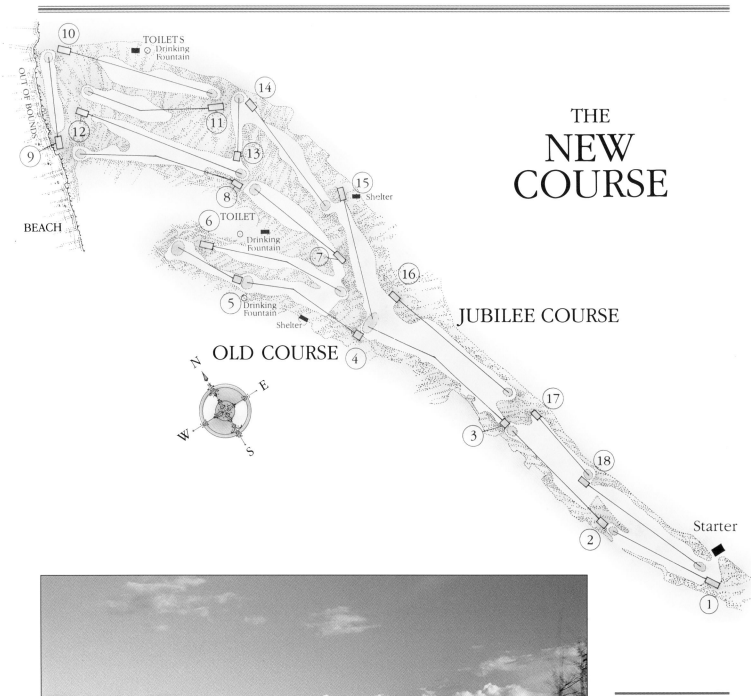

THE
NEW
COURSE

10

TOILETS
Drinking Fountain

14

OUT OF BOUNDS

12

11

9

13

8

15
Shelter

BEACH

6 TOILET

Drinking Fountain

7

5 Drinking Fountain

Shelter

16

JUBILEE COURSE

N
E
W
S

OLD COURSE

4

17

3

18

2

Starter

1

*LEFT Looking back
towards the town from
the New Course.*

The Old Course provided the basis for virtually all course design throughout the world during the frantic period of golfing expansion in the late 1890s and early 1900s, and many of its natural features are still incorporated in modern designs by today's architects. Not unnaturally, the New Course was created in its image, though not slavishly so.

On the plus side is the fact that most bunkers are visible, not hidden. The reverse of the coin is that the face-saving double fairways, which are such a feature of the Old Course, are rare on the New. It is a tighter test of golf for the average player, demanding a higher degree of control to keep the ball in play.

For the professionals to set record scores on the Old Course they must drive the ball with precision into areas from which they can attack the championship pin positions. Yet for the amateur golfer it is very forgiving, with acres of space for wayward tee shots and massive greens to catch the most inaccurate approaches. Thus high-handicap players usually score remarkably well on the Old, but are brought down to earth with a savage bump when they tackle the New, where a tremendous Sunday morning hold-up several years ago was traced to a group of four visiting golfers who had been presented with a dozen balls each by their host before they left the first tee. By the time they reached the eighth hole they had only five balls left between them. Admittedly, the story probably says more about the standard of golf prevailing than the true playing characteristics of the New Course; by comparison with the Old it is certainly a little claustrophobic in places, but it is a fine and fair test of links golf nonetheless.

The difference between the two courses is perfectly illustrated by two holes which run side by side. A poor drive from the sixth tee of the Old will still reach a point opposite the tee of the first short hole, the fifth, on the New. Even with identical distances to the pin on each course, the prospects are totally different. The player on the Old is faced by a deep green which stretches 90 yards to the left as it merges with the twelfth. There is 20 yards of

The fifth green on the New Course offers a narrow target between two bunkers. The sixth green on the Old Course is just out of the picture to the left.

open space to the right and no bunkers in sight. It is possible to miss the pin by 30 yards on either side and still have a good chance of getting a par or, at worst, a five. A few yards to the right on the New Course the shot to the thin plateau green is flanked by sand on either side and surrounded by bushes. Miss the centre of the green by ten yards either way and the ball will finish in a bunker. Miss by 20 yards and it will be lost in the bushes.

There are, however, many holes which offer greater margins for error and there are several points on the course where parallel fairways can save a wayward shot: but these are always separated by cultivated rough, banks of whins, or bunkers. Because the course is played in a clockwise direction these bail-out areas are on the right – a blessing for the player who slices and in direct contrast to the Old Course where, apart from the ninth and tenth, the extra room is always on the left.

The opening holes are deceptively undemanding. Although thick bushes flank more than half of the first fairway on the left, separating it from the Old Course, this is the line to take for a clear pitch to the green between a bunkered mound on the right and further sand on the left edge.

Judgement of distance for the approach to the second is made tricky because the completely flat green is merely an extension of the fairway with no definition between the two. Unusually for a links course, there are trees behind the green to both right and left, but they are too distant to give any real perspective to the shot.

The only double green on the course is shared between the third and the fifteenth holes. At the par-five third a high ridge obscures the right half of the green and a steep bank leads up to the left. A large majority of approach shots kick down and left, short of the putting surface, and it pays to pitch well up into the green.

Thinking golfers will not reach automatically for the driver at the fourth. A ridge runs diagonally across the fairway at the point where it swings gently left, and beyond it the tar-

The fourth green. The approach is from the right of the three bunkers in the foreground.

LEFT The approach to the sixth. BELOW The ninth is a hole that can pose a tough challenge on a windy day.

get area for big hitters gets progressively tighter. The ideal tee shot is one that finishes on top of or just beyond the ridge. The low-lying green has bunkers masking its left side and bushes close behind and to the right.

Comparison has already been made between the short fifth and its next-door neighbour on the Old. The sixth is a longer, reversed version of the fourth, turning to the right and demanding two very good shots to find the small, sharply contoured green.

The straightforward seventh adds a degree of difficulty when the pin is placed behind the deep bunker on the left. This calls for a tee shot down the right edge so that the approach can be aimed in behind the bunker.

To reach the long eighth in two the second shot has to be threaded through a narrow gap in the sandhills with bunkers either side, and the tee shot at the short ninth is no less daunting. The tee is perched high above the waters of the Eden estuary and the green half-hidden in a deep depression in the dunes 220 yards away along the shore. The scene can be idyllic with calm water in the mile-wide estuary and seals basking on distant sandbanks. It can also be ferocious, with wind-blown spray misting the air and pounding water on the left all the way to the green, just waiting to swallow the ball.

167

The inward nine starts with a demanding par four where the semi-blind tee shot must be kept out of the rough-covered humps and hollows that flank the left side; yet the more the ball is kept safely to the right, the more difficult the second shot becomes. Heading back in the opposite direction the eleventh is played to a severely sloping green set back into high dunes and effectively bunkered on both sides.

A drop in fairway height at the only homeward par five can give extra impetus to a well struck drive and bring the green in reach in two. The bunkers left and right are well short of the putting surface.

INSET *The semi-blind drive at the tenth.* MAIN PICTURE *The sloping green of the eleventh; there is another pair of bunkers to the left of the green.*

The tee shot at the par-three thirteenth is probably one more club than most golfers have in their hands, for anything pitching on the front of this deceptive plateau green is likely to slide back down the steep slope.

There is also trouble in selecting the right club for the approach to the fourteenth where a low ridge crosses the entire width of the fairway and hides the dead ground beyond. It can seem that the green is just over the rise, but the pin is likely to be at least 40 yards further back.

The end of the double green allocated to the fifteenth rises sharply up from the fairway and falls away towards the back. To add to the problems it is set at an angle to the line of play. Hitting into the green against the breeze with a long-iron it can be almost impossible to stop the ball and anything falling short is likely to be swept away on the slope into a waiting bunker. Even in calm conditions it takes a beautifully flighted shot to get anywhere near the pin.

The run of tough inward holes continues with a strong par four where the flat green is bunkered short and right and backed by a small clump of stunted trees; and there is little respite at the seventeenth, a so-called one-shotter of well over 200 yards with sand on the right and humps and hollows on the opposite side.

There is no respite at the final hole, where the target area becomes more restricted the further the drive is hit, with broken ground on the right, bunkers down the left, and a series of hummocks and a small bunker cutting across the fairway. The green dips down towards the back, has bunkers on both sides and bushes, mounds and thick rough crawling alarmingly close on the left.

St Andrews is fortunate to have a course of this quality providing a totally different challenge to that thrown down by the Old. Both are true and original links courses, but with entirely different characters. They run side by side over the most famous stretch of golfing country in the world and there is no doubt that the New would have received much wider recognition if it had not been condemned to live in the shadow of the Old.

The sixteenth green is backed by a group of stunted trees.

169

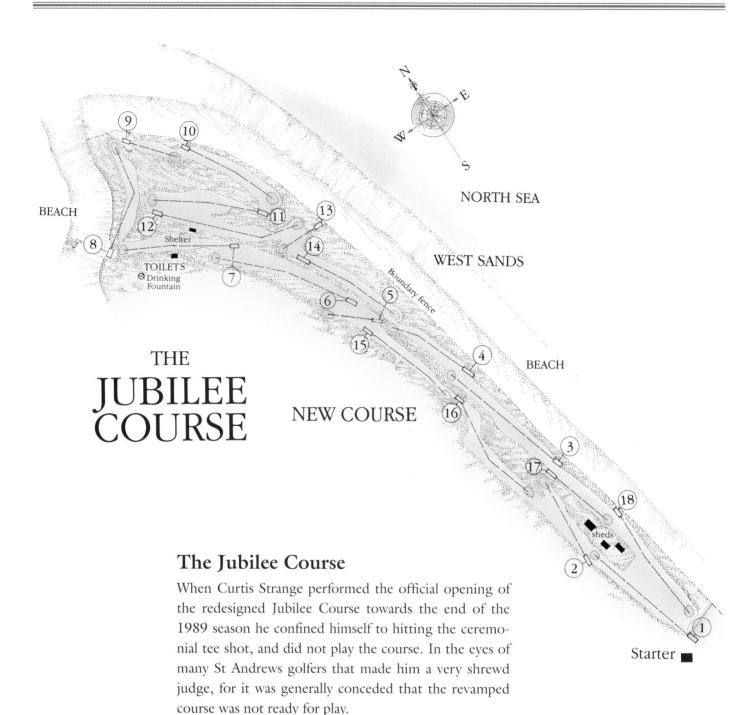

NORTH SEA

WEST SANDS

BEACH

BEACH

NEW COURSE

Boundary fence

Shelter

TOILETS
Drinking
Fountain

sheds

Starter

The Jubilee Course

When Curtis Strange performed the official opening of the redesigned Jubilee Course towards the end of the 1989 season he confined himself to hitting the ceremonial tee shot, and did not play the course. In the eyes of many St Andrews golfers that made him a very shrewd judge, for it was generally conceded that the revamped course was not ready for play.

Sadly, and perhaps because of this premature birth, it remains, six years later, only an immature shadow of the much-vaunted championship course it was supposed to be. Ironically, the drive which Strange hit was at a hole which had been in existence since the course was first built – one of only two holes on the course to remain unchanged in the latest purge.

Built in 1897 (it was named to commemorate Queen Victoria's diamond jubilee), the original course consisted of only 12 holes, but was extended to the full 18 in 1912. Just before the outbreak of the Second World War the R & A's honorary professional, Willie Auchterlonie – who had been Open Champion in 1893 – undertook a fairly wide-ranging reconstruction. His work was not completed until 1946.

The resulting course was of modest length and not too demanding, sheltered in parts by some of the largest sand dunes of the whole links area. It was popular with juniors and with those for whom junior golf was but a distant memory. Ladies loved it, visitors praised it. It was perfect for a morning warm-up before a round on the Old Course or for a few holes on a late summer evening. In short, it brought a further dimension to the game at St Andrews, combining perfectly with the historic qualities of the Old and the tough demands of the New to give a range and variety of golf which catered for all tastes and abilities.

The most recent changes were undertaken in the hope of creating a new championship course which, it was naively thought, would tempt golfers away from the Old Course. That has not happened – and will never happen. Although ten of the original greens are still in use (the Jubilee had gained the reputation of having the finest greens in St Andrews), only two holes remain completely untouched. In some areas holes have been merged, in others they are now played in reverse, and five new holes have been added. Moreover, three of the eight greens which were created in the course of the reconstruction were still out of action five years after the reopening, with temporary greens in use.

Overall, the effect of the redesign has been to make far greater use of the ridge of huge sand dunes which run like a spine through the course. The length of the course has also been massively increased; from being the shortest of the St Andrews courses it has now become the longest, at close to 7,000 yards. The longest, that is to say, available for play by ordinary mortals, since, from the championship tees, the Old Course still has the edge by just over 100 yards. But only occasionally are one or two of these tees brought into play other than during the Open and other major events, and local club golfers and visitors never get to sample the Old Course at full stretch.

There will have been little light left by the time these players on the Jubilee's thirteenth green returned to the clubhouse.

The Jubilee lies closer to the two-and-a-half mile stretch of the West Sands than any of the other St Andrews courses, occupying the area to the east of the New Course, and many of its holes offer fine views along the edge of the bay and back towards the city. The original layout started on the landward side of the ridge of massive sandhills and returned on the seaward side, typical out-and-back links golf. While the new-style Jubilee makes no attempt to return to base at the half-way point, it does switch backwards and forwards through the dunes to produce a richer variety of shots and challenges. Some of the new greens were impossibly tight for a course regularly exposed to strong winds and several have undergone remedial surgery to reshape and extend their putting surfaces.

The green at the second hole, which used to be within reach of a good tee shot, has been pushed back and moulded into the right side of the large dunes, with a bunker cut into the front of the jungle-covered slope. This means that there is absolutely no margin on the left, the ball is either in the bunker, in the rough, in whins on the bank, or on the green. And the other side is only fractionally more forgiving, dropping sharply down towards a shale path and more bushes with a lone, wizened tree overhanging the edge of the green. In a stiff left-to-right wind any second shot that gets more than six feet off the ground is tempting the fates.

The shortest par three on the course is the 162-yard fifth where there is ample room to miss the long, narrow green on the right. But it is certainly a safer option than trying to hold the ball up against the wind and landing in the thick whin bushes on the New Course which lie in wait just off the left rim of the green.

Striking views of the Eden estuary are a bonus from the new tee at the eighth, and it also gives golfers a closer look at the dunes wasteland which borders the left flank of this hole as it turns left towards the sheltered green. The outward half finishes with a totally exposed, long par three from an elevated tee to a crowned green.

Turning for home against a prevailing wind from the right, the second nine is unrelenting. There are back-to-back par fives, five par-four holes, four of which are well over 400 yards, and par threes of just under and just over 200 yards.

From a look at the card the only respite would seem to come at the 356-yard fifteenth. But do not believe everything you read. The landing zone is narrow and tends to throw the ball off to either side. To the right is a rough hollow and a completely blind second shot. To the left lies a bunker and beyond that the ground drops away towards the fourth fairway. The

green is set beyond the bulky shoulder of one huge sand dune on the right and cut into the face of another, with a deep valley between. The original design has been heavily modified – the green considerably enlarged and the row of three bunkers in the driving area reduced to one – but the hole still causes problems out of all proportion to its length. In a way this hole epitomizes the entire course – its potential not quite converted into reality.

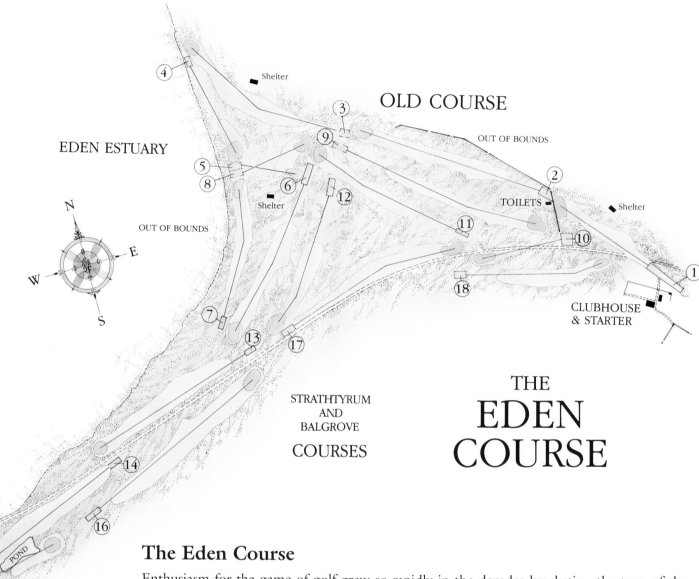

EDEN ESTUARY

OLD COURSE

OUT OF BOUNDS

OUT OF BOUNDS

TOILETS

Shelter

Shelter

Shelter

CLUBHOUSE
& STARTER

STRATHTYRUM
AND
BALGROVE

COURSES

POND

THE
EDEN
COURSE

The Eden Course

Enthusiasm for the game of golf grew so rapidly in the decades bracketing the turn of the last century that in 1912 it was considered necessary not only to expand the Jubilee Course from its original 12 holes to a full 18, but also to build another course.

With no room left between the existing courses and the North Sea, the new Eden Course was constructed on the landward side of the Old, an area of flatter ground, but still true links terrain.

The first tee was established at the closest available point to the town, immediately behind the railway goods yard, now the site of the St Andrews Old Course Hotel, whose other face looks over the seventeenth hole of the Old Course. From this starting point, which was within easy walking distance of all the local golf-club headquarters, the first five holes ran north-west to the mile-wide waters of the Eden estuary, then turned left with a loop of six holes out and back along the shore before heading towards the sanctuary of the town.

Although the Eden shared the same quality of turf and the same links style as the other courses there were far fewer areas of penal gorse and heaving sand-hills. Flatter fairway lies and a greater feeling of spaciousness quickly established its popularity and it became a firm favourite with golfers across the full range of handicaps. The Eden Tournament was inaugurated in 1919 and attracted enormous entries of low-handicap players to take part in qualifying stroke-play rounds before the title was decided by a series of match-play rounds. The event is still held annually, with a higher handicap limit and a lower number of entries, but still attracting golfers from throughout Britain.

For close to 80 years the forgiving fairways of the Eden gave first-time visitors to St Andrews the chance to get to grips with links golf before tackling the Old Course. It was a regular venue for ladies club events and for seniors, but could also offer a challenge full of character to even the best golfers. Yet its popular fairways stood in the path of progress. In order to provide a driving range and practice facilities the official decision was that the Eden must be sacrificed.

The opening and closing holes have now disappeared beneath the thudding balls on the driving range and the course starts at what used to be its third hole. In fact, seven of the original holes came to grief in the shake-up and even some of those that remain were re-shaped in the mistaken quest for additional length.

Luckily common sense finally prevailed at the sixth and seventh holes of the present lay-out. Both were extended and both have now been returned to normality; today they are excellent par fours typical of the original Eden.

In fact, the opening nine holes are all from the original course. The only change is at the first (the third on the original course) which has been slightly extended into a short par four. The incredibly shaped green is raised at the left, with a slight basin to gather the ball, but falls away sharply to a lower level on the right, the whole thing backed by a low, rough stone wall.

INSET *A blustery day on the Eden.*
MAIN PICTURE *The first green is divided into two by a sharp ridge running from front to back.*

From the third tee, especially with a breeze from the west, it is all too easy to make an unintentional appearance on the Old Course, where those waiting on the thirteenth tee are in peril. The hole dog-legs to the right and the line for the tee shot should never be to the right of the guide post. The penalty is severe, for this is one of the few places where encroaching on another course is out of bounds.

The next hole turns along the shore of the estuary and a repeat of the previous tee shot will finish in the water. At low tide the shallow basin empties almost completely and becomes a haven for sea birds.

There is plenty of room to attack the long ninth from the tee, but those hoping to get close to the green in two have bunkers left and right to contend with.

The changes to the Eden caused a great deal of anger and frustration among local golfers, many of whom, in the quieter winter months, play the first nine twice rather than venturing further on to the new holes. Certainly the short tenth is an inauspicious start to the newer parts of the course. Totally devoid of any character or features, the hole has a long, narrow green which has been created by pushing up a mound of earth amid flat surroundings.

It is a relief to get back to another of the old holes at the eleventh where the second shot is played over a bunkered ridge to a raised green. From the fourteenth the course moves into completely new territory and its character becomes noticeably less links-like. This is emphasized by a lake which is the prominent feature of the next two holes, running up the left side of the fourteenth where the new green has been rebuilt in an attempt to stop its evil habit of kicking balls off into the water.

Within three years of the course redesign, the long, uphill sixteenth had abandoned the double green that it shared with the twelfth and moved to new premises further right and heavily mounded on both sides.

The sixth green.

Looking back down the curving fairway of the seventeenth hole, the fence on the left of the picture is out of bounds.

The pick of the new holes is undoubtedly the seventeenth, with thick rough and a large bunker on the left of the driving area and an out-of-bounds fence running all the way to the green down the right flank. The hole swings gently to the right and the entrance to the green is restricted by a bunker on the left and rough rising ground to the right.

The new eighteenth has had to be severely reduced in length to avoid hooked and pulled tee shots endangering players on the tenth and is now a rather insipid drive and pitch hole to a green nestling down amid the whins.

In conclusion, it has to be said that generations of golfers who formed a great affection for the original Eden Course will always question the necessity of ripping out its heart to create practice facilities which could so easily have been built elsewhere.

Looking to the Twenty-first Century

Greater changes have been made to the golfing scene in St Andrews in the final decade of the twentieth century than at any time in the previous 600 years. As already described above, the Jubilee and Eden Courses have been extensively redesigned and rebuilt; the nine-hole children's course has been moved to a different location; a new executive-length course has been opened; and a driving range, practice area, and visitors' clubhouse have been constructed.

177

The executive-length Strathtyrum course has been created on farmland bought from the descendants of George Cheape, the R & A member who stepped in to save the Old Course from disaster in 1821. Unlike the four main courses in St Andrews, the Strathtyrum has no natural features, save a few trees in the area of the first and the eighteenth. The new course has been shaped and moulded from an area of completely flat land, with each green protected by ridges, banks and hollows, some severe and some subtle, and minimal use of sand.

The greens themselves are small and well contoured and each has a very distinct entrance – none of them very wide. In dry conditions, or with a stiff breeze sweeping the course, they are tough targets to hit. Although there is ample fairway space on most holes, a low score will only be achieved by placing tee shots accurately in order to open up the approaches to the greens. The Strathtyrum is a short and pleasant alternative to the more rigorous examination set by the bigger St Andrews courses – ideal as a learning ground and as a course on which to warm-up or wind-down.

The original nine-hole Balgove course, laid out in 1971 principally for children, was swallowed up in the development of the Strathtyrum and has been resited between that course and the driving range. It is still, at times, restricted to use by children and accompanying adults. With virtually no rough or hazards it is a place to learn the basics of the game, a stepping-stone between the practice ground and one of the full-scale courses.

The new practice centre has as its focal point a floodlit driving range; this features both covered and open bays and incorporates areas for instruction, including the use of video equipment. Clubs can be hired. There is also a separate provision for bunker practice and for pitching, chipping and putting.

The completion of a visitors' clubhouse providing locker room and bar and restaurant facilities is the final phase of new development at the Home of Golf. The St Andrews Links Trust believe that they have created the largest and most comprehensive golf complex in Europe to cope with the ever-increasing demand for the game at the place where it all began.

Chapter 12

VISITORS WELCOME

THE DELIGHTFULLY SIMPLE DAYS when anyone with a club and a ball could wander down to the first tee and take their place on the Old Course, unhindered by rules and regulations and without payment, are recalled now only in the pages of history. It is a century since charges for golf were first introduced in St Andrews; the New Course had just opened and summer visitors were charged a fee for its use which today would not go halfway towards the cost of an hour's parking in the town.

The foundations of the management structure which now governs golf in St Andrews were laid in 1894 when an Act of Parliament decreed that the links should be managed by a Green Committee consisting of five members of the Royal and Ancient Golf Club and two individuals appointed by the Town Council. All regulations relating to play on the courses were to be submitted to the Town Council for approval. In this way both the rights and privileges of local golfers and freedom of access to the links for visitors were safeguarded. Subsequently, the most significant change came about in 1974, when a complete restructuring of local government throughout Britain abolished St Andrews Town Council and transferred the links to the larger and more impersonal care of North East Fife District Council. For the first time the links which belonged to the people of St Andrews were owned by an authority based outside the city.

It was at this point that a new Act of Parliament established the St Andrews Links Trust to be legally responsible for the administration and operation of the golf courses. Members of the Trust are nominated by the new local authority, by the R & A, and by the Secretary of State for Scotland. The day-to-day operation of the Trust's policies is handled by a Links Management Committee, with members nominated by the local authority and the R & A. A team of professional administrators is employed by the Committee to implement policy through a staff of some 70 people, including green-keepers, starters, rangers and those handling course bookings.

Fashion may have developed somewhat since the 1950s, but the welcome at St Andrews remains as warm as ever.

181

Booking a Starting Time

With 70,000 golfing visitors a year flooding into the small city, the biggest problem is that demand far exceeds supply, particularly on the Old Course, where the amount of golf played has been dramatically reduced in recent years. Strict opening and closing times have been imposed and starting intervals extended from eight to ten minutes. The course continues to stay closed on Sundays and has an additional month free of play each year, usually two weeks in November and two weeks in March, for rest and maintenance.

One of the joys of St Andrews used to be early-morning and late-evening golf on the Old Course in the summer months. At a latitude slightly north of Copenhagen, Moscow, and Edmonton, daylight arrives well before 4.00 am and lingers past midnight. Many local golfers were accustomed to getting in a round before breakfast or after dinner. The new regulations and the ever-decreasing speed of play now make this impossible; they have also prevented one St Andrews golfer from continuing to tackle his annual challenge of playing a round on each of the four main courses in one day of golfing gluttony.

There is only one certain way to get a game on the Old Course and that is to book in advance. Payment of green fees must be made in full at the time of booking and golfers making an advance reservation in this way must also book and pay for a round on one of the other St Andrews courses. There is also a chance of getting on the Old through the daily ballot. This operates like a giant lottery. Names are submitted to the starter or the links office, either in person or by telephone, before 2.00 pm for the following day's play. Applications for Monday play must be made on Saturday. At 4.00 pm the results of the day's draw are posted at the starters' boxes, in local golf clubs and in the Tourist Information Office in the centre of town. Golfers who have travelled thousands of miles to the Home of Golf can be seen scanning these lists as if their lives depended on the outcome.

Failure to get on to the starting sheet through the ballot leaves only one other course of action. Check with the starter in his little box by the first tee. He will do his best to match you up with a two- or three-ball, but it probably means hanging around ready to go at a moment's notice. St Andrews golfers are, however, kindly folk and will usually invite a frustrated visitor to join in. An invitation to share a little wine of the country in one of the golf clubs that look out over the eighteenth fairway usually follows. The New and St Andrews Golf Clubs both welcome male visitors on a daily temporary-membership basis, giving them use of club facilities.

The starter's box on the Old Course.

All visitors playing the Old Course must have a handicap certificate or a letter of introduction from a recognized golf club. Caddies are available throughout the year. Payment is made to the caddie-master before play and is passed on to the caddie when the round is successfully completed. In summer months golf trolleys are usually allowed on the Old Course after midday, but this is a concession that is always subject to withdrawal.

Starting times for the Jubilee, Eden and Strathtyrum courses can be booked at the links office a day in advance, but the New and Balgove operate purely on a first-come, first-served basis. On the New Course priority is given at certain times to local golfers.

All enquiries about playing golf at St Andrews should be addressed to: The Links Trust, St Andrews, Fife, KY16 9JA. Tel. 01334 475757.

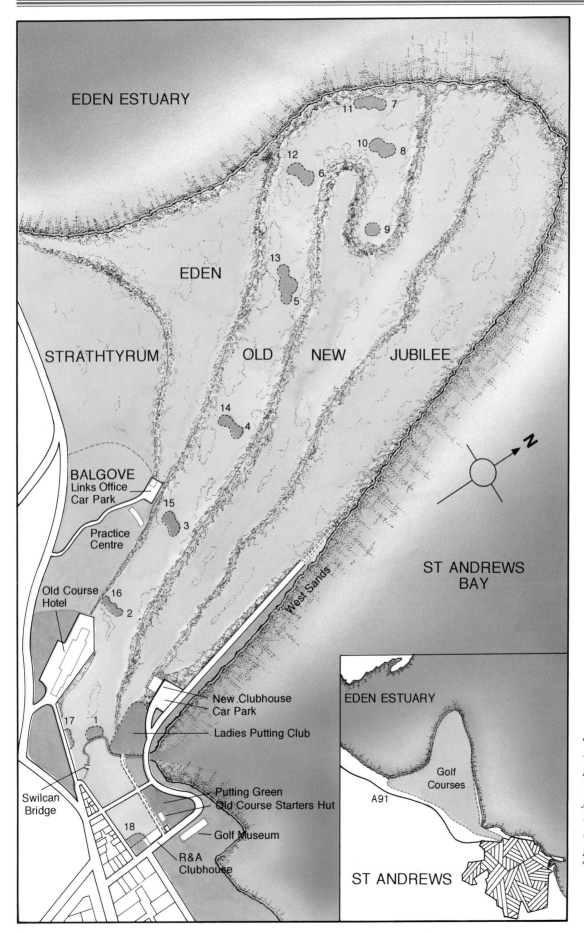

EDEN ESTUARY

11 7

10 8

12 6

9

EDEN

13

5

STRATHYRUM OLD NEW JUBILEE

14

4

N

BALGOVE
Links Office
Car Park

15

3

Practice
Centre

ST ANDREWS
BAY

Old Course
Hotel

16

2

West Sands

New Clubhouse
Car Park

EDEN ESTUARY

17 1

Ladies Putting Club

Golf
Courses

Swilcan
Bridge

A91

Putting Green
Old Course Starters Hut

18

Golf Museum

R&A
Clubhouse

ST ANDREWS

A golfer's paradise is packed into the peninsula which separates the city from the Eden estuary to the north. This map may be compared to the aerial photograph on page 20.

183

Year-round Golf

It is never a good idea to arrive in St Andrews hoping for a game on the Old Course without checking in advance. The Royal and Ancient hold their spring and autumn meetings in March and September when the Old is booked for their sole use for several days at a time. Other local clubs have traditional bookings for their championships and the Dunhill event takes another week out of the calendar in October. With a heavy list of advance bookings there can be, at times, very few slots available for the ballot.

Demand for times drops off from November to April and, despite the city's position on the east coast of Scotland, golf is possible, and often very pleasurable, in St Andrews throughout the year. Most winters pass with no snow to interfere with activity on the links, though frost can delay the start of play, the final green on the Old Course being the last to free itself from the shadow of the surrounding buildings and shake off the icy fingers. But in general St Andrews benefits from its own micro-climate. The wet weather that sweeps in from the Atlantic usually races along the Clyde-Forth valley, by-passing St Andrews to the south, and the wide expanse of the River Tay performs a similar service to the north. Standing on the eleventh green in brilliant sunshine while heavy clouds drench the streets of Dundee just a few miles away is a common experience.

Hot summer days, however, can often be followed by periods of thick 'haar'; this is a sea mist which rolls over the sands and creeps slowly over the courses while a few hundred yards

Golf is possible throughout the year – almost.
INSET *The Himalayas, used by the Ladies Putting Club, with the Old Course Hotel in the background.*

further inland the countryside is still bathed in sunshine.

Temperatures are always unpredictable and it is just as possible to enjoy a round of golf in one-sweater sunshine in December as it is in July; but, generally, winter days tend to be bright and sunny, with a bracing edge to the air. Yet when the winter wind swings around to the north-east, picking up speed over the vast expanses of Siberia and Scandinavia before venting its full spleen on the exposed links, hardened local golfers still fight their way to the far end of the ancient links – pausing only to sip frequently from well-filled hip flasks.

No matter what the weather, if the Old Course is open, there will be golfers pitting their skills against its timeless qualities. It can be beautiful and brutal, ferocious and frustrating, inspiring and infuriating – all on the same day.

Getting There

The ancient Kingdom of Fife is shaped rather like the head of a dog, thrusting its nose into the cold waters of the North Sea towards Denmark, cut off to the south by the wide waters of the Firth of Forth and to the north by the turbulent currents of the River Tay. St Andrews, set on the point of this promontory, does not lie on any of Scotland's main trunk routes, but this has never stopped visitors in their thousands flocking to its broad streets. They came, at first, to seek spiritual solace from the relics of St Andrew; then to attend Scotland's oldest university; and today, in ever increasing numbers, to force the world's most famous golf course into submission.

St Andrews is little more than an hour away from Edinburgh by car, and just under two hours from Glasgow. The station at Leuchars Junction provides access by railway.

In fact, despite the city's relatively isolated position, access is not difficult. From Edinburgh, the M90 motorway takes you over the Forth Road Bridge, with its spectacular views, past the hundred-year-old rail bridge to the open sea, heading due north to Perth. The A91 road to St Andrews, which is well sign-posted, leaves the motorway shortly after you have passed Loch Leven on the right. The small island castle where Mary Queen of Scots was held prisoner is visible from the road; it was here, in July 1567, that she was forced to renounce her throne.

By road, the journey from Edinburgh takes little more than an hour. The capital can be reached by road, rail or air; there are regular flights from London and an increasingly comprehensive service from Europe. But many transatlantic flights terminate at Glasgow, some 45 miles west of Edinburgh. From there to St Andrews by car is a journey of just under two hours.

The railway branch-line that once ran right through the heart of the golf courses into St Andrews was abandoned in the late 60s and Leuchars Junction is now the nearest point on the rail network. Trains from Edinburgh reach

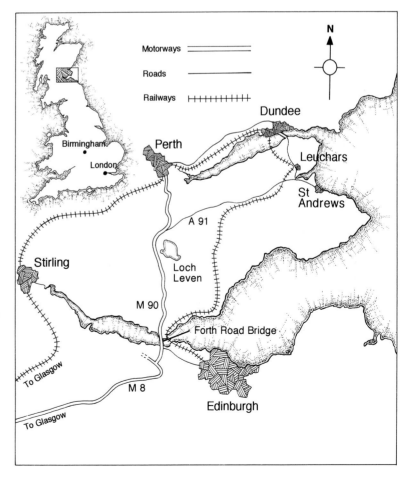

Leuchars in about an hour. The train journey from Glasgow, via Dundee, takes approximately twice as long. The road from Leuchars links up with the main approach from the motorway and brings golfers into the city along the flat coastal plain, with the ancient spires clearly visible in the distance. At night the floodlit facade of the Royal and Ancient clubhouse seems to float out of the darkness. The golf courses are in clear view on the left of the road and a side turning

by the driving range takes golfers directly to the Links Trusts offices and information centre. A large car park gives access to the range and practice area and also the Eden, Strathtyrum and Balgove courses. Those eager for a glimpse of the Old Course should continue into the city, taking the first turning left after the stone bulk of Rusacks Hotel, into Golf Place. Within 50 yards the buildings on the left come to an abrupt end to reveal the most keenly anticipated vista in golf. Beyond the eighteenth green and the wide sweep of the first and last fairways the Old Course curls away to the right, half hidden by the rising dunes and the new links clubhouse, with a ridge of sand hills running into the distance separating the ancient links from the shoreline.

Beyond St Andrews

The St Andrews courses by no means exhaust the golfing possibilities of the region. The magnificent championship course at Carnoustie is just 45 minutes away by car. This is one of the toughest and most challenging courses on which the Open has ever been played and it was here that Tom Watson won the first of his five Open titles in 1975. After a gap of 24 years, the course is due to host the Championship again in 1999.

An hour's drive away through the magnificent scenery of Glen Devon lies Gleneagles where the three famous courses – the King's, the Queen's and the new Monarch's, which has been designed by Jack Nicklaus – are open only to those who stay in the magnificent hotel.

Nearer at hand for the visitor to St Andrews are other, more modest, courses which can provide a welcome change of pace. To the south lies the old seashore layout of Crail, founded in 1786 and thus one of the oldest clubs in the world. Here there are wonderful views from every hole, but a couple of steep climbs along the way.

The nearby Lundin Links course also has one steep hill to negotiate, climbing away from the links holes by the shore to a more parkland-type setting for a few inland holes. This course once ran all the way along the edge of the sea, but was split in two many years ago, the other half forming the basis of Leven's excellent links. Once a year the boundaries are opened up and a competition played over the original course.

Directly inland from St Andrews, just off the main route back to the motorway, is Ladybank: an exquisite course set amid pine and heather where the fine, sheltered golf is particularly appealing when the links courses are being swept by cold winds.

Just to the north of the Home of Golf, the Scotscraig course at Tayport is also laid out on fine crisp turf bordered by heather and trees. Renowned for its immaculate condition it adds another dimension to golf in the Kingdom.

St Andrews Golf Clubs

In 1995, the Links Trust opened its imposing new clubhouse for use by all visitors but particularly useful for those playing the Old, New and Jubilee courses. The clubhouse has a full range of locker room facilities, plus bar and restaurant. At the Eden course complex only basic changing rooms are available.

For those who prefer the use of a well established club, both the St Andrews Club, which was founded in 1843, and the New Club, which dates from 1902, offer temporary membership to visiting male golfers, allowing them to make use of their facilities for a minimal daily fee.

The St Andrews Club, which has Jack Nicklaus as an honorary member, overlooks the final green of the Old Course and is a highly competitive club with a large proportion of its members in single figures. The club also plays host to the Thistle Golf Club, founded in 1817 and, after the R & A, the oldest club in St Andrews, where the large membership plays annually for a vast array of wonderful trophies.

The New Club lies mid-way between tee and green of the eighteenth. Here, Arnold Palmer is the celebrated honorary member, and a superb new dining room set high above the last fairway provides one of the most spectacular settings for a summer dinner.

Visitors who would like temporary membership of either club should write in advance of their visit, simply addressing their letter to one or other of the clubs, at St Andrews, Fife, Scotland.

The two ladies clubs – St Rule and St Regulus – do not have sufficient accommodation to offer temporary membership to visiting ladies; but both have thriving memberships taking part in full programmes of competitions.

The oldest ladies club was established on a small corner of the links close to the first green on the Old Course by wives of R & A members in 1867. In those days there was a great deal of scepticism about women playing golf and it was not considered proper for them to raise the club above the shoulders. This rather genteel form of pitch and putt has come a long way

OVERLEAF *The Old Course Hotel seen from the Swilcan Bridge.* INSET LEFT *The British Golf Museum.* INSET RIGHT *A typical St Andrews 'haar'.*

An artist's impression of the new visitors' clubhouse, due to open its doors in 1995.

187

The Ladies' Putting Green dates back to the 1860s, when it was considered improper for women to raise the club above shoulder level. The ladies in this nineteenth century photograph are clearly playing very safe!

in the intervening years, but the Ladies' Putting Club, as it is now known, still flourishes on the same piece of ground. It is the only part of the links which is not under the direct control of the Links Trust and the club's lease has recently been extended until the year 2016. Because of the severe undulations over which their extensive putting green is laid out, the area has been known for many years as the Himalayas. It is open to the public and lengthy queues form throughout the summer months.

There is also a public putting green on the Bruce Embankment beside the first tee of the Old Course, laid out on ground reclaimed from the sea when a barrier of old fishing boats was sunk to keep the high tides away from the first fairway and create an access route to the West Sands which did not involve crossing the Old Course.

Close to this putting green and immediately behind the R & A clubhouse the British Golf Museum has been created. Making full use of audio-visual aids as well as stunning collections of clubs, balls, trophies, equipment and golfing memorabilia, it traces the full, fascinating history of the game.

Hotels, Restaurants and Bars

A stay in St Andrews can be enjoyed in the grand style, or on a budget. Accommodation ranges from a choice of small friendly bed-and-breakfast establishments to the expensive opulence of the grand hotels. The choice of food on offer ranges from excellent bar meals in the majority of the town's pubs to establishments specializing in steak and chicken and Italian, Chinese and Indian restaurants. Fine quality Scottish meat and vegetables and superb, cold-water fish and shellfish are available in a wide variety of restaurants, ranging from those offering superbly good value to the budget-conscious, to others which will tempt the visitor to epicurean indulgence.

Bars abound, all of them resonant with golfing chatter, catering to every kind of customer, from those dying for a pint of ale after a four-hour round to those who prefer to perch on a high stool sipping a very dry martini while trying to decide between the lobster and the chateaubriand, to be followed, perhaps, by a dram or two and the enjoyment of good Scottish hospitality, no different from the 'Nobles and Gentlemen' who started it all in 1754.

INDEX

191

The author and publishers wish to thank the following for permission to reproduce photographs: **St Andrews University Photographic Collection**, pp. 12, 15, 16, 36 (insets), 39 (inset), 44 (bottom), 48 (bottom), 50, 55, 56 (right), 57 (right), 60-1, 63 (inset), 64, 68, 70, 71 (bottom), 72 (right), 73 (bottom right and left), 75, 76 (inset), 78 (centre), 80 (bottom), 90, 96 (left), 97, 98, 99, 100, 101, 105 (bottom), 109 (bottom), 111 (bottom), 114, 119, 125 (left), 126 (right), 131, 180, 190; **Hobbs Golf Collection,** pp. 6, 10, 13 (top), 14, 21, 27, 28, 30, 31, 33, 36 (main picture), 37, 39, 40, 42, 43, 44 (top), 45, 46, 47, 48 (top right and left), 51, 52, 56 (left), 57 (left), 58, 59, 62, 63 (top), 64 (inset), 66 (bottom), 67 (bottom), 69, 71 (top), 72 (left), 73 (top), 74, 76, 78 (insets), 79 (bottom), 80 (top), 81, 82, 83, 84 (right), 85 (inset), 85 (top left, top right and bottom), 87 (inset), 88 (bottom right), 92 (top), 93, 94 (inset), 95, 96 (top right and inset), 102, 104, 105 (top), 107, 108, 109 (top), 110, 112, 115, 116-17, 118, 120, 122, 125 (right), 126 (bottom), 127, 128, 129, 161 (inset), 164, 188 (inset), 189 (inset right); **Whiteholme of Dundee**, p. 32; **David J. Whyte/Golf-Photo-Library** (tel. 01382 643656), pp. 2-3, 8, 13, 19, 20, 22, 23, 24-5, 34-5, 49, 66 (top), 129, 132, 134, 136, 139, 145, 146, 148-9, 158, 160-1, 162, 165, 166, 167, 168, 169, 171, 172, 173, 175, 176, 177, 178 (inset top), 178, 179, 182, 184, 186, 188-9; **Matthew Harris/The Golf Picture Library,** pp. 86 (top), 87 (top and bottom), 88 (top and inset), 89, 90 (inset), 92 (middle, bottom right and left), 130, 138, 143, 151, 156.

Maps are reproduced by kind permission of the following: pp. 183 and 185 © **Ken Lewis**; pp. 135, 137, 138, 140, 141, 142, 144, 145, 146, 147, 150, 151, 152, 153, 154, 155, 156, 157, 159, 164, 170, 174 © **David J. Hogg/St Andrews Links Trust.**